FLEECING THE FLOCK

SETTING THE PEOPLE OF GOD FREE FROM THE LIES OF TITHING

"EACH ONE MUST DO JUST AS HE HAS PURPOSED IN HIS HEART, NOT GRUDGINGLY OR UNDER COMPULSION, FOR GOD LOVES A CHEERFUL GIVER." 2 CORINTHIANS 9:7

ANTHONY WADE

FLEECING THE FLOCK

Setting the People of God Free From the Lies of Tithing

Anthony Wade

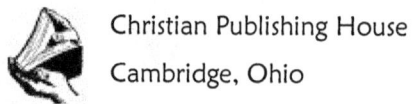

Christian Publishing House
Cambridge, Ohio

Christian Publishing House
Professional Conservative Christian
Publishing of the Good News!

Copyright © 2018 Anthony Wade

All rights reserved. Except for brief quotations in articles, other publications, book reviews, and blogs, no part of this book may be reproduced in any manner without prior written permission from the publishers. For information, write,

support@christianpublishers.org

Unless otherwise indicated, Scripture quotations are from the Updated American Standard Version of the Holy Scriptures, 2016 edition (UASV).

FLEECING THE FLOCK: Setting the People of God Free From the Lies of Tithing

Authored by Anthony Wade

ISBN-13: **978-1-945757-96-9**

ISBN-10: **1-945757-96-5**

Table of Contents

CHAPTER ONE Foundational Truths and the New Testament Model of Giving 1

CHAPTER TWO The Lie of Never Naming Names 11

CHAPTER THREE The "Judge Not" Lie 19

CHAPTER FOUR The General Tithing Lie 33

CHAPTER FIVE The Malachi Lies 43

CHAPTER SIX The Abram & Jacob Tithed Lies 73

CHAPTER SEVEN The Jesus Taught Tithing Lie 79

CHAPTER EIGHT The Seed-Sower Lies 83

CHAPTER NINE The Hebrews Confirms Tithing Lie 91

CHAPTER TEN The First Fruits Lie 103

CHAPTER ELEVEN The Cursed Money Lie 113

CHAPTER TWELVE The More Absurd Lies 119

CHAPTER THIRTEEN Debunking Common Arguments 129

CHAPTER FOURTEEN Assemblies of God Tithing Position 134

CHAPTER FIFTEEN The Hate the Church Lie 142

CHAPTER SIXTEEN A Way Forward 151

Bibliography 157

Anthony Wade

CHAPTER ONE Foundational Truths and the New Testament Model of Giving

I remember the night. It was a Friday night prayer service at my church, and there was a guest speaker. His name was Bishop Ken McNatt. I had been saved several years and been through most of my Berean Bible courses towards earning my ministerial credentials but in many ways was still very naive. Not so much naive in terms of doctrine as much as with Churchianity. I still believed everyone was in this for Christ and His cause. The little dog had not yet pulled back the curtain, so I had yet to see who the wizard really was.

To be honest, Bishop McNatt brought a powerful, relevant Word. I remember it was in the Old Testament and I was taking notes furiously. When the Word ended, however, is when the lunacy began. You see it was time for the offering. Now I am not against offerings at all. I believe a workman is worth his wages. Back then I was also faithfully tithing as I had been taught. I was in a good church, however. A church with a Pastor who faithfully brought the unvarnished Word of God every night. A Pastor who tried his best to keep out the influences of the world. As such, despite the fact that I knew the charlatans on TBN were not worth my time, I had never seen hucksters in person.

2 Corinthians 2:17 Updated American Standard Version (UASV)

[17] For we are not, like so many, peddlers[1] of God's word, but as men of sincerity, as commissioned by God, in the sight of God we speak in Christ.

Then I saw Bishop McNatt. He was given the microphone to do his own pitch for the offering, which was to go to his "ministry." He began the pitch by telling a story he said happened to him the previous week at another church. That God had "told him" that there were ten people in the congregation ready to "sow" a $300 "seed." He claimed that as he was about to pray over the people who came forward for their $300 miracle, a little old lady pushed her way to the front and begged to be prayed for as well, even though she did not have the requisite $300 on her. She promised she would bring the $300 first thing Monday morning to the church. McNatt said that he included her in the prayer and that week she

---

[1] A deceptive greedy business person, a tavern keeper, or a wine merchant, a petty retailer, a huckster, a peddler.

came in and gave the church three times the amount because she had come into a windfall thanks allegedly, to the prayer. Glory hallelujah - pass the offering plate.

As I listened, my mind was racing to sort through the various theological problems with this story. First the notion that God instructed him to only pray for people with $300 seemed ridiculously unbiblical and preposterous. Secondly, however, he wanted me to believe that he then disobeyed that command and God blessed it anyway? By the time I looked up in my disbelief he was making the same pitch to my church. My family. He made people run up to the altar and throw their money on it for him. To be honest, a more disgusting display I had never seen in church. The altar of God covered in money given by people trying to buy blessings from a snake oil salesman of the highest order. My innocence died a bit that night as I realized that not everyone is in this for Jesus. Not only that but some of those charged with guarding the door to the sheep pen are actually wolves seeking to devour that which has been entrusted to them. I should have known. Paul had warned us about this:

Acts 20:29-30 Updated American Standard Version (UASV)

²⁹ I know that after my departure fierce wolves will come in among you, not sparing the flock; ³⁰ and from among your own selves men will arise, speaking twisted things, to draw away the disciples after them.

Since that fateful Friday night, God has continued to pull that curtain back and expose the lies and corruption running roughshod through His church. In no bigger area do we see leaven in the body of Christ than when it comes to giving. Not all of the leaven is as easy to spot as Bishop McNatt, and even though his sham was obvious to me, he easily got his desired $3,000 that night from my church family. Within the realm of giving, one of the biggest lies that enslaves so many of God's people is the lie of tithing. It is interesting to note that one of the biggest complaints Protestant believers have about Catholicism is that it is largely based on ritual and not the Bible yet that is exactly the argument most tithing Protestants make about the tithe. It's just how we were raised. It is just what we were taught. Does that matter? Absolutely not. The only thing that matters is the truth of God found in His Word. That really is supposed to be our foundation beloved.

2Timothy 3: 16-17 Updated American Standard Version (UASV)

¹⁶ All Scripture is inspired by God and profitable for teaching, for reproof, for correction, for training in righteousness; ¹⁷ so that the man of God may be fully competent, equipped for every good work.

What we allow to lead us is what we worship. The truth is there are too many carnal Christians today. The new models of church growth create them. Too often we worship the pastor, or we even worship the church itself. That is actually how a cult begins; when the pastor or leader is worshiped instead of God Almighty. I love my pastor dearly, but he did not die for me. He cannot save me. Any pastor worthy of the mantle they take will always point you back to Jesus. Read these Timothy verses. Only the Bible is divinely written. It is breathed out directly by God. It teaches us, corrects us, rebukes us, trains and equips us. This is where we always must start. This is where we must always end. This is where we must always be found. False teaching is specifically false because it disagrees with something in the Word of God. False prophets are specifically false because they are in disagreement with the Word of God. The Apostle Paul wrote about all sorts of problems the early churches were having. We see pastor worship, church worship, and outright heresies embraced. Yet when he came to Berea he found people he called more noble. What made them more noble was that they checked what he taught them against Scripture to make sure they were being taught correctly. We need more Bereans these days. Christians who will search the Scriptures to make sure they are being taught correctly. Instead, what we see are hyper-defensive Christians who will misuse Scriptures to protect their favorite false teacher. It doesn't matter if they are being robbed blind by these people. Because their foundation is not Scriptural, it is carnal. It is time for Christians everywhere to take off the shackles they so willingly clamp onto their lives and breathe the fresh air again. Now I know the hucksters can be very convincing. I know they have large followings. But spiritual success is not measured with carnal metrics. Just because Joel Osteen packs 50,000 into Yankee stadium does not mean God is in on it. God uses the foolish to confound the wise. In this book, we are going to walk through every popular tithing argument that is made and show biblically why they are simply wrong.

It is important here to note that I am not speaking of motives or intent. One of the usual non-biblical arguments is, "you can't judge their heart!" I do not have to judge their heart. It does not matter what their intent was. As my pastor is fond of saying, you can be sincere and also be sincerely wrong. The Bible, however, says I am to judge their fruit. I am to evaluate their teaching. I am to do the noble work of a Berean. Along with intent a quick note about the usage of the word "lie." A lie is simply put a falsehood. Sometimes the definition can go as to say it must be intentional. I do not go that far. When I refer to something being a lie, I am merely saying it is not true. Once again, it may not be speaking directly to intent. I can live with the thought that Joel Osteen thinks he is serving God. I can live with the thought that he wakes up every day and believes he is doing good. In a temporal way, he does a lot of good. In an eternal way, however, he is as false as they come. This is not because of his heart but rather because of his teaching. Also, we need to realize that not everything a false teacher says or believes is false. This is another ridiculous standard applied too often. Wolves do not walk into a congregation with a neon sign around their neck, and many wolves may not even know they are in fact a wolf. A favorite "Christianism" often utilized is that we must "eat the meat and spit out the bones." I disagree. If I know the bone is rotten, why in the world would I trust the meat? What we support is what other people then see we support. What we re-tweet and post on Facebook matters.

1 Corinthians 10:23-24 Updated American Standard Version (UASV)

[23] All things are permissible, but not all things are advantageous. All things are lawful, but not all things build up. [24] Let each one keep seeking, not his own good, but that of the other person.

We are instructed not to cause our brothers and sisters to stumble. When we repost the daily status of a teacher or prophet we know to be false, we are in fact endorsing them. People see us repost and assume that is tacit approval. Our witness for Christ must be paramount. Before we get into the specific biblical arguments against what is being taught, it would be wise if I address what is sure to be the top criticism against a book such as this. Inevitably, when you start talking about the truth regarding tithing, you will be accused of trying to cheat God. That you "just don't want to give" or that you are "cheap" in some manner. That people get "funny when you talk about their money." It is all a distraction of course because they know they are wrong biblically. Either way, however, allow me to clear the air right now. I do believe in giving to the church. In fact, I believe in it more than the average person who pays tithes. I believe there is no bigger investment that we can make than a kingdom investment. When we find a church that is faithfully bringing the whole and uncompromised Gospel of Jesus Christ the Holy Spirit inside of us should rise up to want to pay into the efforts of that church for the glory of God and the advancement of His kingdom! Here is the hard truth, however - that is not tithing. That is New Testament giving. Instead, what do we see today?

> *God is a businessman. He is not going to do business with someone who shows no sign of potential return.* - TD Jakes

> *There's a reason you can't keep your kid out of the hospital.* - Perry Noble

> *"Yes, the church wants your money!! Guess what? It's not your money! God gave you that money, Big Boy! My name is Steven Furtick, and I approve this message!"* - Steven Furtick

So according to "Bishop" Jakes, God is a businessman who will not invest in you unless He is assured that you will guarantee some form of financial return unto Him? Are you serious? According to Perry Noble, God is striking your kid with sickness because you are not giving according to what he wants? Are you serious? The only one who came close to the truth here was Furtick when he admitted what is really going on - the church wants your money! I checked with God before I wrote this. He assures me He is not short on cash. All Biblical teaching about money shows it to be a tremendous stumbling block to our relationship with God yet it seems those in charge of the flock haven't received that message.

The tithing deception, however, is far from limited to those who are false. It has been taught for centuries. Even the most well-intended and biblically sound pastors still preach tithing. They do so because it is what they know and deep down there is fear that abandoning it will result in plummeting resources needed to keep their church doors open. Let's examine that for a moment. The hard reality is the majority of churches today no longer preach the full counsel of God. Biblical exposition has been replaced by diabetic, topical motivational speeches designed to make people feel better about themselves when they really need to feel worse about themselves and better about God. They then implement a ridiculous sinner's prayer system, which grants absolution without repentance as the pastor proclaims the individual saved based upon three sentences. The result as Paul Washer once said, 'you end up with a congregation filled with goats, and you try to teach them to act like sheep.' What's the relationship to giving? The New Testament model for giving does not work without the help of the Holy Spirit.

John 16:13-15 Updated American Standard Version (UASV)

[13] But when that one, the Spirit of truth, comes, he will guide you into all the truth; for he will not speak from himself, but whatever he hears, he will speak; and he will declare to you the things that are to come. [14] That one will glorify me, for he will take what is mine and declare it to you. [15] All the things that the Father has are mine; therefore I said that he takes what is mine and will declare it to you.

Without the Spirit of God, the things of God remain foolishness to those who are perishing, regardless of whether they go to church. So if you leave giving up to goats, you will not receive much I would imagine, which is why the false love tithing. It gives them the ability to demand a certain portion and blame it on God. The truth is if you left giving up to solid biblical preaching and the indwelt Holy Spirit - you would get more than 10%. Pastors sell God short and show an incredible lack of faith to preach tithing. Many pastors do realize this truism. The perpetuation of forced tithing is grounded in a lack of faith in God by the pastor. So what is the model for New Testament giving? As you may have guessed, it is found in the New Testament:

2 Corinthians 9: 6-7 Updated American Standard Version (UASV)

6 Now as to this, he who sows sparingly will also reap sparingly, and he who sows bountifully will also reap bountifully. 7 Each one must give as he has decided in his heart, not reluctantly or under compulsion, for God loves a cheerful giver.

This is it beloved. It is not rocket science. It is not some deep theological construct you need three different biblical translations to grasp. We often make God more mysterious than He really is. These verses are the model for New Testament giving. It starts with the general principle of sowing and reaping. As we sow, so shall we reap. What makes this a general principle, and not just in money, is that it is fully corroborated by the entire canon of Scripture:

Proverbs 11:24 Updated American Standard Version (UASV)

24 One man scatters[2] freely, yet grows all the richer;
  another withholds what he should give, and only suffers want.

Galatians 6:7-8 Updated American Standard Version (UASV)

7 Do not be deceived: God is not to be mocked, for whatever a person sows, this he will also reap. 8 For the one who sows to his own flesh will from the flesh reap corruption, but the one who sows to the Spirit will from the Spirit reap eternal life.

As I said, if you are in a solid, Bible-based church that preaches the full counsel of God, then giving to the work of that church will become the most important investment you make. The Bible teaches to store up treasures in heaven, not here on earth. Only things that are eternal have eternal value and as Don Henley once sang, there are no hearses with luggage racks.

The next lesson from the model shows that we must decide what it is we will give. Not the church. Not your pastor. We must place a value on what we get from our church. How well we are fed and how well they are preaching the Gospel? We need to pray and then give as God leads us to give. Perhaps this week God leads us to give ten percent. Perhaps next week He says to pay down our debt first. Perhaps the week after He directs us to give nearly everything we have. If the church has a need God may direct

---

[2] The Hebrew verb (pā·zăr) means to scatter: to spread, to distribute, to give to another implying generosity, a figurative expression of sowing seed

us to meet it. If there is a congregant that has a need, God may direct us to meet it. The church is a building, but we are the Body of Christ. James teaches us:

James 2: 15-17 Updated American Standard Version (UASV)

[15] If a brother or sister is without clothes and lacks daily food, [16] and one of you says to them, "Go in peace, be warmed and be filled," and yet you do not give them what is necessary for their body, what good[3] is that? [17] Even so faith, if it has no works, is dead in itself.

We all know these verses, but we live the hypocrisy far too often. We see our brothers and sisters in need and say something trite and worn out. Some vague Christianism we have learned over the years. We tell them to have faith when what they need is a hot meal. We tell them God is able when they need a warm coat. We tell them we will pray for them instead of stopping our lives long enough actually to pray with them. We think that "As you did for the least of them" is a great sounding bumper sticker but not a practical way to lead a life. Why? Often, this is because we think we have done our duty. We have been "faithful" in our tithe. We wield it like a "get out of Christian responsibility" card. That is not how God saw New Testament giving.

We then see that God gives us two conditions that must *not* be part of the equation. The first is that we must not give reluctantly. God does not want our money as much as He wants our hearts fully committed to Him and the work of the kingdom. If you are going to give and then regret the giving - God does not want it. The Bible tells us a story about this:

Mark 10:17-22 Updated American Standard Version (UASV)

[17] And as he was setting out on his journey, a man ran up and knelt before him and asked him, "Good Teacher, what must I do to inherit eternal life?" [18] And Jesus said to him, "Why do you call me good? No one is good except God alone. [19] You know the commandments: 'Do not murder, Do not commit adultery, Do not steal, Do not bear false witness, Do not defraud, Honor your father and mother.'" [20] And he said to him, "Teacher, all these I have kept from my youth." [21] And Jesus, looking at him, loved him, and said to him, "You lack one thing: go, sell all that you have and give to the poor, and you will have treasure in heaven; and come, follow me." [22] But at these words he was saddened, and he went away grieving, for he was one who had many possessions.

---

[3] Or *benefit*

Money is not the root of all evil. The love of money is. The problem the rich young ruler had was not his wealth but that he valued his wealth over God. It was getting in between him and God. Sometimes we can be like this young man as well. We can think we are doing all the right Christian duty. We are obedient to the commandments as best we can and repent when we sin. Yet when it comes to giving to the work of the kingdom, we can be as reluctant as this rich young ruler. Paul is laying out for us that reluctant giving is simply not the model. The reality is tithing often results in reluctant givers.

Which brings us to the second condition, which is God does not want our giving to be compulsory. This is a bottom line proof that tithing is not biblical. The dictionary defines compulsory as something that is required. That is the very definition of the nature of tithing as it is taught today. One cannot just walk away from this Scripture without concluding that enforcing tithing is UNBIBLICAL. It creates a compulsory giving system which then violates 2 Corinthians 9:7. God loves a cheerful giver - not a coerced giver. God wants people to be invested in the work of the kingdom; not just financially but with their hearts as well.

I had written about this before and received some expected pushback from faithful tithers. A quick word to those in this system already. If you feel led to give 10% there is nothing wrong with that. That does not make it "tithing." I have had good brothers and sisters swear that "tithing works." They usually offer up some story of faithful deliverance by God such as their job being saved from downsizing or an unexpected financial blessing that came right on time. My answer to that is found in the words of the Christian author Edward D. Andrews,

> If we ever find ourselves in difficult times, unrelenting times, we need to follow the pattern set by the Psalmist (Psalm 42:4-6). We need to remember that God is well aware of our circumstances, and he will not forsake us.
>
> **Proverbs 3:25-26** Updated American Standard Version (UASV)
>
> [25] Do not be afraid of sudden panic[4]
> or the storm of the wicked, when it comes,
> [26] for Jehovah will be your confidence
> and will keep your foot from being caught.
>
> What do these verses mean? Should we understand that these verses or any others in Scripture teach that because we are wisely walking with God that he will miraculously step in to protect each servant personally

---

[4] Or *fear, dread, terror*

from difficult times, diseases, mental disorders, injury or death? No. These sorts of miracles are the extreme exception to the rule. Of the 4,000 plus years of Bible history, from Adam to Jesus, with tens of millions of people living and dying, we have but a few dozen miracles that we know of in Scripture. Even in Bible times, miracles were not typical, far from it. Hundreds of years may pass with no historical record of a miracle happening at all.

If we are wisely walking with God, we can be confident that bodily disease, mental disorders, injury or early death are far less likely than if we were not. Moreover, we can draw on the resurrection hope. Does God miraculously move events to save us out of difficult times or miraculously heal us? Yes, he certainly can, but it is an extreme exception to the rule. He miraculously heals those who are going to play a significant role in his settling of the issues that were raised in the Garden of Eden.

What God's Word teaches us is this, that if we walk by using discernment and exercising sound judgment from Scripture, unless unexpected events befall us, we can be sure that we will not stumble into the difficulties that the world of humankind alienated from God faces every day. Conversely, the wicked do not have this protection as they reject the Word of God as foolish. In other words, Christians live by the moral values of Scripture, which gives them an advantage over those who do not. Therefore, God answers our prayers by our faithfully acting on behalf of those prayers, by applying Scripture in a balanced manner. If we have not taken in a deep understanding of God's Word, how can we have the Spirit-inspired wisdom, the very knowledge of God to guide and direct us in our ways? Just because we are not being rescued when we feel that we should, this does not mean that we have lost faith, or that God is displeased. Even though the Psalmist had no doubt that Jehovah God was coming to his aid, he still experienced grief ... If we are to remain rational in our thinking, we need to grasp the fact that God does not always step in when we believe he should, nor is he obligated to do so.[5]

---

[5] Does God Step in and Solve Our Every Problem Because We are Faithful? http://bit.ly/2qLdxgN

We are bound by sowing and reaping. So if you are a faithful giver into the work of the ministry, who also regularly and consistently reads, studies, and applies the Word of God, it does not surprise me that God would protect you or give you some level of favor (although He is not bound to), if that is according to his will and purposes. So it is not that "tithing works." It is that you are obediently following the Lord in giving and probably in most other areas of your life and thus you see the results of that. Sowing and reaping remain a universal principle. Tithing remains a lie.

CHAPTER TWO The Lie of Never Naming Names

It sometimes seems we who are called to divide the Word of God lose our focus. We lose our sense of priorities. I understand the desire to be protective over whom we might view as our own. Sometimes ministry can be exasperating. Sometimes it can seem as if everyone is against you. Sometimes it seems as if we are required to play by a different set of rules than everyone else. As if more is required of us.

James 3:1 Updated American Standard Version (UASV)

3 Not many of you should become teachers, my brothers, knowing that we shall receive heavier judgment.

That is because more is required of us! And amidst the daily grind of life and the business ministry can often become, let us not lose sight of what this is about. It is not about me. It is not about you. It is not about Joel Osteen, Benny Hinn, or any other public ministry figure. It is about Jesus. While that is true, it is about even more than Jesus. It is about the Gospel of Jesus Christ. While that is true, it is about even more than the Gospel of Jesus Christ. It is about the eternal destination for the souls of men. It is not about your best life now. It is not about building a purpose driven church. It is not about erecting million-dollar arenas, having 50 ministries, and getting a show on TBN. It is about the crack addict sitting in your last pew. It is about the single mother, pregnant again and homeless. It is about the average everyday person who is still on the outside of salvation looking in. Because at the end of the day it is not about their addiction, their pregnancy or their seeming "normalness" – it is about the simple fact that they are separated from God and are destined for an eternity in hell.[6] I know these aren't the flowery messages we hear any more from the seeker friendly pulpits, but this is the truth. There is a heaven, and there is a hell and standing in the gap between them are the ministers of the Gospel of Jesus

---

[6] While Christian Publishing House (CPH) is publishing Fleecing the Flock, they would adamantly disagree with the author on the hellfire doctrine. CPH's position is that the hellfire doctrine of eternal torment is unbiblical. Below are some free online CPH Blog articles for the reader, so he or she can have both sides, so as to make an informed decision for themselves.

Hellfire – Eternal Torment? (http://tiny.cc/pmnwsy) What Did Jesus Teach About Hell? (http://tiny.cc/7hnwsy) Is Hellfire Part of Divine Justice? (http://tiny.cc/gnnwsy) Is the Hellfire Doctrine Truly Just? (http://tiny.cc/0nnwsy) The Bible's Viewpoint of Death (http://tiny.cc/9nnwsy) Do Humans Have a Soul that Is Apart From Us? (http://tiny.cc/4onwsy).

Christ. That Gospel must be bigger than any one of us. It must be bigger than all of us. When did we become so thinned skin that any legitimate criticism is met with such derision? If we cannot tolerate correction for vital portions of doctrine, how in the world will we tolerate real persecution?

Matthew 24:9 Updated American Standard Version (UASV)

9 "Then they will deliver you up to tribulation, and will kill you, and you will be hated by all nations because of my name.

How are we leading people to stand during the coming persecutions? In other countries, ministers are forced to hide underground, share scraps of the Gospel, and die for their beliefs but we get upset because we think someone has said something mean about us? I write this as a backdrop to the issue known in Christian circles as "naming names." This comes up seemingly whenever there is something really offensive to the true Gospel put forth by someone who had been considered sound doctrinally or commands a large portion of the Christian audience. In the inglorious past of Pentecostalism, known apostates such as Paul Crouch would call us "heresy hunters." Infamous heretic Benny Hinn once said he wished he had a "holy ghost machine gun" so he could blow these people away. What people? People who would dare question the fact that he is an operative of Satan, exploiting Christianity for his own personal profit. More recently, we have seen people like Mark Driscoll, who is no stranger to stretching the Gospel beyond what it was written for, whine in sermons about people who dare question him. Soon after he would fall from grace.

For the record, we are talking about matters of crucial doctrine, not petty matters reasonable people can disagree about. I prefer that people talk about what they have in common – not what separates them. But there has to be a dividing line. There has to be a line we refuse to cross when it comes to the integrity of the Gospel message. While I understand why those who are facing the truth about their own heresies would bristle, I am amazed at the defenders they have. We are supposed to contend for the faith – not the flesh. We are supposed to defend the Gospel – not the preachers. In this age of watered down churches have we fallen so far away that we minimize the importance of the Gospel? Have we arrived at the point that we really think that everyone in a church is going to heaven? That a simple two sentence prayer is all that is required? That we don't have to get into the dos and the don'ts? That we think as Osteen, that doctrine is a dirty word that "weighs people down?" That it is more important to place people into ministry than into the Kingdom? Do we really think that any old Gospel message will do as long as we think we are "reaching them for Christ?" Allow me to remind us of the severity in which we operate:

1 Corinthians 15: 1-2 Updated American Standard Version (UASV)

15 Now I make known to you, brothers, the gospel which I proclaimed to you, which you have also received, in which you also stand, ² by which you are also being saved, if you hold fast to the message I proclaimed to you, unless you believed in vain.

Take this next question very seriously beloved. Upon what Gospel are we taking our stand? Look at what the Apostle Paul is saying here! It is only by the actual Gospel that people are saved! Otherwise you have believed in vain! How many people sit in the pews every week believing in vain? Goats trying to act like sheep. Do we hold firmly to the Word or do we nod and wink and look the other way? How loose is our hold on the Gospel message today? I dare say it is quite loose and growing looser every day. When we think that it is more important to defend man over the integrity of the Gospel I would say that it is not just loose – it has fallen to the floor.

Dear Lord just look at what we have accepted in the body of Christ! Rob Bell once led a congregation of 15,000 people and now he thinks hell doesn't exist! Mark Batterson is teaching people to redo their prayer life based upon a fictional, non-biblical character who petulantly dismisses the sovereignty of God! The Easter Bunny on the altar of God so we can appear "relevant" to a dying culture! Prosperity preachers milking the body for cash in the name of Jesus. Faith healing frauds and false signs and wonders disguised as a "move of the Spirit." Jesus Culture indoctrinating our youth with nonsense not seen since the Holy Laughter debacle of the 1990's. Self-help and motivational speaking passed off as Christianity. Grace alone doctrine designed to tickle the ears and consign countless to hell. No fear of God. No reverence before God. Gold dust, gem stones, angel feathers and glory clouds. This isn't a game. The eternal destination of the souls of men hang in the balance and we need to treat it like so. It does not give me any pleasure to name names. I am comforted however that the Bible clearly indicates that we are in fact supposed to call out by name those who would preach a Gospel contrary to the truth.

2 Timothy 2:15-18 Updated American Standard Version (UASV)

¹⁵ Do your best to present yourself to God as one approved, a workman who does not need to be ashamed, rightly handling[7] the word of truth. ¹⁶ But avoid empty speeches that violate what is holy, for they will lead to more and more ungodliness, ¹⁷ and their word will spread like gangrene; Hymenaeus and Philetus are among them. ¹⁸ men who have

---

[7] Or *accurately handling* the word of truth; *correctly teaching* the word of truth

gone astray from the truth saying that the resurrection has already taken place, and they upset the faith of some.

Expositing these verses start with a simple statement we all need to remember every day as ministers of the Gospel. Work hard so we can present ourselves to God for His approval. There is so much meat there. It starts with working hard. No one said this calling was going to be easy. But look at WHY we work hard. We do not work hard to be approved by man. We do not work hard so we can expand our congregations and build bigger churches. We do not work hard so we can have a television show or write a bestselling book. We work hard so that God might approve of us:

1 Corinthians 2:1-5 Updated American Standard Version (UASV)

2 And I, when I came to you, brothers, did not come with superiority of speech or of wisdom, proclaiming to you the testimony of God. ² For I determined not to know anything among you except Jesus Christ and him crucified. ³ And I was with you in weakness and in fear and in much trembling, ⁴ and my message and my preaching were not in persuasive words of wisdom, but in demonstration of the Spirit and of power, ⁵ so that your faith would not rest on the wisdom of men, but on the power of God.

This is Paul explaining to the Church at Corinth how we are supposed to approach the preaching of the Word of God. Not relying upon eloquence, human wisdom, or persuasive words. The object isn't to trick people into the kingdom because it doesn't work that way. It is neither by might nor strength but by the Spirit of God only! Do we resolve to know nothing before those we speak except Jesus Christ and Him crucified? Do we even talk about the crucifixion anymore? Besides Easter? Are our messages covered in the blood or do we avoid the messiness of true salvation at all costs? Is our greatest hope that visitors come back or that they are saved? Remember, some plant and some water but only God gives the increase.

Next in the 2 Timothy verses we see that we should absolutely be ashamed if we do not correctly explain the Word of God. Please, I am not talking about perfection. I am not talking about inconsequential disagreements. If this one prefers hymns and that one prefers modern worship that is fine as long as it brings glory to God. If this one believes in being slain in the Spirit and that one doesn't, fine. Why? Because no one is going to remain unsaved because they believe in being slain or they do not. But someone who says a quick and dirty prayer without the weight of the burden of their sin driving them to repentance? Sorry, but all the seeker friendly nonsense in the world is not sending that person to heaven. Jesus

Christ is our Savior. That means He needed to save us from something. That something is not cultural irrelevance or a life of insignificance. That something he saves us from is our SIN. He saves us from the one thing that separates us from God! How do we lose sight of that so easily? Because it is not preached anymore. Instead we see churches routinely engaging in foolish, worthless talk that only leads to more godless behavior. Sermons designed to make people feel better about themselves when they need to feel better about God. Beloved – if this is our best life now then by definition we are going to hell.

When carnality is what is embraced in the pulpit then carnality is what is being taught. Naming names is how you stop the foolish and worthless talk. Turning a blind eye to it does not serve Christ. The verses from 2 Timothy warn us very plainly that talk like this spread like cancer. Don't believe what God is saying here? Just look at the seeker friendly, purpose driven model in America. The vast majority of churches embrace this over the Gospel. Well intended pastors defend the need to be relevant to the community they are in as a means to justify the secularization of their churches. The Apostle Paul visited Greek cities that would make modern day San Francisco blush in their decadence. Did he ever once try to be relevant to the dying culture? Of course not. The church is supposed to be different – not relevant. We are supposed to be a peculiar people, not a similar people. We are supposed to be pilgrims and sojourners, not residents.

We see in these verses from 2 Timothy that the Apostle Paul does in fact name names! He specifically mentions two people – Hymenaeus and Philetus. What was their crime? Heresy! They were preaching a different Gospel than they had received! How crucial is this to God? How important is the purity of the doctrine to our God?

Revelation 22:18-19 Updated American Standard Version (UASV)

[18] I testify to everyone who hears the words of the prophecy of this book: if anyone adds to them, God will add to him the plagues which are written in this book; [19] and if anyone takes away from the words of the book of this prophecy, God will take away his part from the tree of life and out of the holy city, which are written in this book.

Beloved, it is not what we say that saves anyone but what God says. Our fancy buildings, community outreaches, and creative ministries save no one. I once heard a mega-church pastor say that because of the new plasma flat screen TV's in the basement, three youth gave their lives to Christ one Friday evening. Those are some powerful televisions! It is silly of course. It is actually worthless talk that spreads like cancer. It is so important to God that if anyone dares to add anything to the Gospel message then all of the curses that appear in the entire Bible shall apply to that person!

Why is all of this important? Why does God name names here? What is the end result of the heresy of Hymenaeus and Philetus? They have turned some people away from the faith. Remember, this is not about you or me. It is about Jesus Christ and the unsaved masses of people out there looking in on our salvation. They probably turned away some good people. Some God-fearing people. Some people with great intentions. Beloved realize that it gives me no pleasure to say that Joel Osteen is a false teacher. It gives me no pleasure to say that Joseph Prince teaches a false Gospel. Or that The Circle Maker is heretical teaching. But Osteen, Prince, and Batterson are big boys. I am worried about the hundreds of thousands of people who attend their churches or follow them and think they are saved when they are not. People who have taken their stand on a compromised Gospel with a watered-down Christ who saves no one. There are 45,000 people who attend Osteen's church every week. Is it possible that some are introduced to God for the first time through his work? Sure, but realize God does not use false teachers. If one's heart is receptive to the truth, God will make certain that he or she is introduced to that truth sometime in their life by those carrying out the work of an evangelist. Mind you, all true Christians are evangelists, so it could be anyone of us who introduce the truth to these lost ones. Their best life is not now; it's still out there waiting for them. Waiting for someone to preach the actual Gospel of Jesus Christ to them!

Romans 1:16-17 Updated American Standard Version (UASV)

[16] For I am not ashamed of the gospel, for it is the power of God for salvation to everyone who believes, to the Jew first and also to the Greek. [17] For in it the righteousness of God is revealed from faith for faith, as it is written, "The righteous shall live by faith."

The Gospel is not meant to help us become relevant. It is not meant to help us feel significant. It is meant to tell us how God makes us right in His sight! It is no surprise that these verses are written to Timothy, who was a pastor in charge of his own church. In his first letter to Timothy, Paul explained the close relationship between what we preach and the salvation of those who would hear us:

1 Timothy 4:16 Updated American Standard Version (UASV)

[16] Pay close attention to yourself and to your teaching; persevere in these things, for as you do this you will ensure salvation both for yourself and for those who hear you.

Undeniably, if we are to help others get on the path of salvation, we must first pay attention to ourselves and our teaching. True Christianity thus stands in stark contrast with false Christianity, many of which seek to manipulate the thinking of their members as they twist the Scriptures. The salvation of those who hear what is preached is always on the line. If you think by the way that this naming of names was a onetime event, you would be wrong:

2 Timothy 1:15 Updated American Standard Version (UASV)

15 You know this, that all who are in[8] Asia[9] turned away from me, among whom are Phygelus and Hermogenes.

On this, Knute Larson writes, "When Paul had lived in Ephesus, so many people had received the gospel that the message of Christ spread throughout Asia (Acts 19:1–20). Since that time, the arrest of Paul and the rise of false teachers had weakened the church and shaken the faith of many. Perhaps, under the circumstances, they supposed Christianity was a failed enterprise. Whatever the cause, a dramatic shift of faith had occurred."[10]

2 Timothy 4:10 Updated American Standard Version (UASV)

10 for Demas, having loved this present world,[11] has deserted me and gone to Thessalonica; Crescens has gone to Galatia, Titus to Dalmatia.

We turn to Bible commentator Knute Larson again, "**Demas ... has deserted me.** Being alone does not always create a sense of loneliness, but being deserted almost certainly will. Desertion has betrayal as its root. Nothing strikes at the heart of a person more than violated trust. Demas was one of the apostle's friends and associates; Paul mentioned him in Colossians 4:14 and Philemon 24, describing him as a "fellow worker." He seems to have served faithfully with Paul, Luke, and others in the missionary endeavor. Yet, in the end, he abandoned Paul and the work **because he loved this world.** In a few words, Paul penned a double tragedy: not only was Paul abandoned, but Demas had forsaken the goodness of the gospel. Two men suffered loss, though Demas's was more lasting. Demas probably did not deny Christ and march off to Thessalonica in defiant arrogance. He does not appear as a heretic, signing on with the false teachers. Instead, Demas seems to exhibit the human tendency to seek personal safety. He probably traded in the values of God for the values of this world—the

---

[8] Or *for*

[9] Or *wholesome; healthful; beneficial*

[10] Knute Larson, *I & II Thessalonians, I & II Timothy, Titus, Philemon*, vol. 9, Holman New Testament Commentary (Nashville, TN: Broadman & Holman Publishers, 2000), 271.

[11] Or *age*

values of immediacy. He probably still believed in Christ, but he was unwilling to endure hardship, to identify with the imprisoned apostle and his unpopular teachings. His heartstrings were attached to personal protection and comfort. This can easily happen to us who live in the affluent Western cultures. One more thing about Demas: he began well. Faithful service and zealous work do not guarantee the future. Our lives must be lived faithfully each day, each week, year upon year. Here was a man who had served Christ well, who had belonged to an intimate circle of workers with the apostle Paul, and yet he abandoned it in the end. Demas serves as a warning to each of us that we cannot rest on our past or assume the future. We must maintain steady diligence in the present moment. In addition to Demas's desertion, **Crescens** had gone to **Galatia**, and **Titus** to **Dalmatia**. These were fellow workers who had proceeded to other locations to continue work in established churches, perhaps even to plant new congregations. Paul found nothing wrong in their travels, but their departure magnified his loneliness.[12]

2 Timothy 4:14-15 Updated American Standard Version (UASV)

14 Alexander the coppersmith did me great harm; the Lord will repay him according to his deeds. 15 Be on guard against him yourself, for he vigorously opposed our words.[13]

The Alexander connected with Hymenaeus was guilty of a very serious wrong, blasphemy, and both of these men were expelled from the church, handed over to Satan as it were so that they were no longer able to contaminate or influence the early Christian congregation. For convincing reasons, then, Christians should have a personal Bible study daily, seek the truth and constantly pray for the courage necessary to resist any infringement on the pure worship of God. As we progress here, I will not hesitate to call out those who deserve to be called out for the false Gospel they preach because that is exactly what the Bible says we are to do.

---

[12] Knute Larson, *I & II Thessalonians, I & II Timothy, Titus, Philemon*, vol. 9, Holman New Testament Commentary (Nashville, TN: Broadman & Holman Publishers, 2000), 323–324.

[13] I.e., *teaching*

CHAPTER THREE The "Judge Not" Lie

Matthew 7: 1-5 Updated American Standard Version (UASV)

7 "**Do not judge** so that you will not be judged. ² For with the judgment you are judging you will be judged, and by what measure you are measuring, it will be measured to you. ³ Why do you look at the speck that is in your brother's eye, but do not notice the log that is in your own eye? ⁴ Or how will you say to your brother, 'Let me take the speck out of your eye,' and look, the log is in your own eye? ⁵ You hypocrite, first take the log out of your own eye, and then you will see clearly to take the speck out of your brother's eye.

Matthew 7:1 King James Version (KJV)

7 **Judge not**, that ye be not judged.

Matthew 7:1 American Standard Version (ASV)

7 **Judge not**, that ye be not judged.

Matthew 7:1 Young's Literal Translation (YLT)

7 `**Judge not**, that ye may not be judged,

Matthew 7:1 The Greek New Testament, Fourth Revised

7   Μὴ   κρίνετε, ἵνα   μὴ   κριθῆτε·

Not judge   that not you might be judged

Now that we have established some foundational truths and addressed the biblical clarity to name names, it is prudent to prepare for the inevitable criticism; the accusation of judgment. Contrary to what many professing Christians seem to believe, "judge not," is not a Bible verse. It is first two words spoken by Jesus from the Sermon on the Mount. The KJV, ASV, YLT, and the ESV render it very literally as "judge not," while the other literal translations (UASV, NASB, CSB, LEB) insert a verb "do" (third person present) to complete the sense in the English text, as "do not judge." The Greek verb (*krinō*) is an imperative, which means that it is a command or exhortation. Most who use this phrase are ripping it violently out of the context in which it was meant to be used. Let's be honest too. It is probably one of the top "Christian" phrases used by both saved and unsaved. "Judge not" is a Christian defense mechanism used primarily for two reasons. The first is to not have to hear about our own sin and the second is to defend our favorite false teachers/prophets.

When it comes to sin we, all know the drill. Someone has the temerity to point out to a brother or sister that he or she is in sin and the reflexive response is "don't judge me" or "who are you to judge!" The truth, of course, is that we are our brother's keeper. If not us, then who? The problem is not the fact that someone tells us we are sinning. The problem is we are sinning, and when we sow to the flesh, we will always reap destruction. What does the Bible specifically say about our responsibility here? Let's take a moment and look at a few commentators on this often misunderstood and misused small phrase "judge not." Stuart K. Weber writes, "This is one of the most often misunderstood and misquoted passages in all the Bible. It is important to understand that Jesus was not making a blanket prohibition against all judgment and discernment, but only against that which is done in self-centered pride. A good summary of his meaning is, 'Do not judge others until you are prepared to be judged by the same standard. And then, when you exercise judgment toward others, do it with humility.'"[14]

Leon Morris writes, "*Do not judge* refers to the passing of harsh, adverse verdicts on the conduct of our fellows; it does not forbid the use of our best critical thinking (which may be done in a spirit of tolerance and helpfulness and which Jesus elsewhere commands as a help to others, 18:15; for that matter how can we avoid casting pearls before pigs [v. 6] without a process of discrimination?). 'Don't judge' does not mean 'don't think' (Stott remarks that the command 'is not a requirement to be blind, but rather a plea to be generous,' p. 177). The verb is used not only generally of passing a verdict, but specifically of passing an adverse verdict, condemning, and it is this that Jesus is forbidding. The present imperative gives the sense 'Don't make a practice of judging.'"[15]

Really Jesus was not suggesting that we do not judge others in the sense of analyzing or evaluating them as being worthy of our Christian association or for us to be able to assist them in recovering from serious sin but rather Jesus was talking about being overly critical in a condemnatory manner. On this Craig Blomberg writes, "'Judge' (*krinō*) can imply *to*

---

[14] Stuart K. Weber, *Matthew*, vol. 1, Holman New Testament Commentary (Nashville, TN: Broadman & Holman Publishers, 2000), 96.

[15] Leon Morris, *The Gospel according to Matthew*, The Pillar New Testament Commentary (Grand Rapids, MI; Leicester, England: W.B. Eerdmans; Inter-Varsity Press, 1992), 164–165.

analyze or *evaluate* as well as *to condemn* or *avenge*. The former senses are clearly commanded of believers (e.g., 1 Cor 5:5; 1 John 4:1), but the latter are reserved for God. Even on those occasions when we render a negative evaluation of others, our purposes should be constructive and not retributive. So Jesus is here commanding his followers not to be characterized by judgmental attitudes (cf. Williams, 'Stop criticizing others'). The immediate practical rationale for his command is that others, including God, may treat us in the same manner we treat them. Verse 2 provides the premise for v. 12."[16]

What if a brother or sister of our Christian congregation is "strays from the truth," deviating from the right teaching of God's word and conduct?

James 5: 19-20 Updated American Standard Version (UASV)

[19] My brothers, if any among you strays from the truth and one turns him back, [20] let him know that he who turns a sinner from the error of his way will save his soul from death and will cover a multitude of sins.

Therefore, it is clear that we can and should judge our brothers and sisters (as well as unbelievers too) in the sense of analyzing or evaluating them as being worthy of our Christian association or for us to be able to assist them if they have "strays from the truth," or helping them in their recovery from serious sin. We do so through Bible counsel, prayer, and other help. A Christian who turns a wrongdoer back from a sinful course, or stumbling out of the faith, saves the soul of the repentant person from spiritual shipwreck and perhaps from eternal destruction. – 2 Thessalonians 1:9' 2 Peter 3:7.

Yet we remain so gifted at providing Christian sound bites rather than sound doctrine. Another favorite here is when people say, "let he without sin cast the first stone!" (John 8:7, KJV) While that sounds so righteous, it actually is merely one line in a much larger story. Moreover, it comes from a spurious passage that was not a part of the original text. (John 7:53–8:11) However, because of its early history, it can be spoken of here. The Pharisees had caught a woman in the act of adultery. They were not trying to restore her. They were not trying to bring her back from her wandering. They wanted to stone her to death. More specifically, they were trying to trap Jesus into speaking against the Mosaic Law. So, if your argument is that we should not try and stone people we find in sin, I wholeheartedly agree and more importantly, Scripture agrees. But that does not mean we ignore

---

[16] Craig Blomberg, *Matthew*, vol. 22, The New American Commentary (Nashville: Broadman & Holman Publishers, 1992), 127.

the sin. That is essentially what the "judge not" crowd advocates and that is not even supported by this story:

John 8:10-11 Updated American Standard Version (UASV)[17]

[[[10] Jesus stood up and said to her, "Woman, where are they? Did no one condemned you?" [11] She said, "No one, Lord." And Jesus said, "Neither do I condemn you; go, and from now on sin no more."]]

No one is advocating for condemning a sinner because we all fall short of the glory of God. We are all sinners. But the convenient part people tend to leave out is when Jesus says; go and sin no more. Wait a minute preacher! The Book of James says who are you to judge your neighbor! Yes, it does, but what is the context?

James 4:11-12 Updated American Standard Version (UASV)

[11] Do not speak against one another, brothers. He who speaks against a brother or judges his brother, speaks against the law and judges the law; but if you judge the law, you are not a doer of the law but a judge. [12] There is only one lawgiver and judge, he who is able to save and to destroy. But who are you to judge your neighbor?

There's a little more here than merely don't judge your neighbor. The context reveals that James is clearly dealing with speaking evil against your neighbor. Other translations refer to this as slander. Commentaries agree that this is when someone is providing false reports or false testimonies about someone. So again, if your point is that we should not provide false witness against our neighbors; I wholeheartedly agree.

The sad ironic thing is that we get things so backward in the church. We are constantly judging the world. They are sinners. They are heathens. They are going to hell. Look at what they are doing to this country. They

---

[17] John 7:53–8:11 is included in NA[28] and UBS[5] enclosed within double square brackets. WH has it after John's gospel. It is included in TR as 7:53–8:11. The following witnesses **omit** 7:53–8:11, P^{39vid} P^{66} P^{75} ℵ A^{vid}, B, C^{vid} L N T W Δ Θ Ψ 0141 33 it[a,f] syr[c,s,p] cop[sa,bo,ach2] geo Diatessaron Origen Chrysostom Cyril Tertullian Cyprian MSS[according to Augustine]

The following witnesses **included** 7:53–8:11, D (F) G H K M U Γ it[aur,c,d,e] syr[h,pal] cop[bomss] Maj MSS[according to Didymus]; E 8:2-11 with asterisks; Λ 8:3-11 with asterisks; f[1] after John 21:25; f[13] after Luke 21:38; 1333[c] 8:3-11 after Luke 24:53; 225 after John 7:36.

We have added into the footnote, not the main text because it is a spurious passage. Single brackets [ ], are used to indicates that the translator(s) had difficulty in deciding which variant to place in the text. Double brackets [[ ]], are used to indicate a spurious passage that has been added to the text. However, because of its early history, it has been included within double brackets.

have taken prayer out of schools and the Ten Commandments out of courthouses. Christians then hold up signs in protest, telling them God hates them. Then an avowed Christian fall into sin and the collective cry is - Judge not! Let us set the record straight biblically:

1 Corinthians 5:12-13 Updated American Standard Version (UASV)

[12] For what do I have to do with judging those outside? Do you not judge those inside? [13] But those who are outside, God will judge. Remove the wicked man from among yourselves.

Those in the world are facing the judgment of God. We are not supposed to shout about their sins but rather shout about He who can save them from their sins. On the other side, we are supposed to deal directly with the sin in our own camp. If we dig further into the context of 1 Corinthians 5 we will see that the church at Corinth was turning a blind eye to someone who was committing sexual sin with the wife of their father.

1 Corinthians 5:1-2 Updated American Standard Version (UASV)

5 It is actually reported that there is sexual immorality[18] among you, and immorality of such a kind as does not exist even among the Gentiles, that someone has his father's wife. [2] And you are arrogant[19] and have not mourned instead, so that the one who had done this deed would be removed from your midst.

This is what we do today in the church. Maybe not the same exact sin but the same exact response. Blind pious arrogance in the face of what God hates. Let us be honest beloved. We simply do not mourn over our sin at all. We pay lip service to it. We seek out churches that will refuse to even talk about it. And if it happens to be pointed out by anyone we scream - judge not! Let us now exposit the whole context of the judge not verses to see exactly what Jesus is trying to say to us. Working backward in these verses we begin with the core revelation we all need to grasp:

Matthew 7:3-5 Updated American Standard Version (UASV)

[3] Why do you look at the speck that is in your brother's eye, but do not notice the log that is in your own eye? [4] Or how will you say to your brother, 'Let me take the speck out of your eye,' and look, the log is in

---

[18] **Sexual Immorality**: (Heb. *zanah*; Gr. *porneia*) A general term for immoral sexual acts of any kind: such as adultery, prostitution, sexual relations between people not married to each other, homosexuality, and bestiality. – Num. 25:1; Deut. 22:21; Matt. 5:32; 1 Cor. 5:1.
[19] Lit *puffed up*

your own eye? ⁵ You hypocrite, first take the log out of your own eye, and then you will see clearly to take the speck out of your brother's eye.

That's right. These verses are not addressing judging. They are addressing hypocrisy. Jesus is not saying we are not to judge. In fact, it is clear from this portion that He is saying we should judge! We should help our brother with the speck that is in his eye. We just should not do it when there is a log in our own. What does that mean preacher? That means if I am in an adulterous affair I should not be judging my brother's adulterous affair. Wow! Let that revelation sink in for a moment. Jesus understands our depraved nature so well. God understands our sinful state so well. It is so much easier to pick on other people rather than deal with ourselves. It is so much easier to call someone a sinner than look at our own sin. The miserable wretch that I am must first look in the mirror and remove what splinter might be lodged there before turning to my brother to help him with the speck in his eye. This is the essence of physician heal thyself. It also encapsulates the correct order of things for us as Christians. It reminds us that Mary has chosen the better thing. Our walk with the Lord must come first in every area of our life. Is it important to help our brothers and sisters? Is it important to spread the truth and light of the Gospel? Is it important to draw a line in the sand against sin and evil? All answers are a resounding yes but not before we first ensure we have removed the logs from our own eyes. Not that we would be perfect but rather that we not be hypocrites. We must remember that whatever we think is hidden in the darkness God will bring to light. So what good does it do to spread the Gospel and then be exposed in an adulterous affair? What good does it do to rail against the sins of the world while you are secretly committing them in private, only to be exposed at some point? What good do we think we are doing by correcting our brother or sister for a sin they know full well we are still wrapped up in? We do more harm than good. We finish with the verses from Matthew:

Matthew 7:1-2 Updated American Standard Version (UASV)

7 "Judge not, that you be not judged.[2] For with the judgment you pronounce you will be judged, and with the measure you use it will be measured to you.

So, we come to it. Judge not, that you be not judged. But it is far more involved than simply that. Jesus did not intend for this to be a sound bite to wield as a hammer, smashing any attempt to correct sin. We can tell just from this immediate context that it is the manner in which the judgment is pronounced. The discussion of another's sin should never be from a place other than love. It cannot come from a motive other than love.

Galatians 6:1-5 Updated American Standard Version (UASV)

6 Brothers, even if anyone is caught in any trespass,[20] you who are spiritual, restore such a one in a spirit of gentleness; each one looking to yourself, so that you too will not be tempted. ² Bear one another's burdens, and so fulfill the law of Christ. ³ For if anyone thinks he is something, when he is nothing, he deceives himself. ⁴ But each one must examine his own work, and then he will have reason for boasting in regard to himself alone, and not in regard to another. ⁵ For each one will bear his own load.

The object is not to develop a critical spirit, searching for sin in everyone we meet. The object is to love one another so much, that when we see a brother or sister falling away, we would be motivated to restore them as an outpouring of that love. That restoration is a gentle process beloved. It stems from a place of understanding where that other person is and what they might be going through. It is easy to simply pronounce judgment and lord it over the person, but that is not bearing one another's burdens. We bear one another's burden by understanding what those burdens are. Understanding the weight of them and the severity of carrying them. Not that we can physically bear them ourselves - verse five indicates we cannot. Yet we should be striving to understand the burden before we judge the sin.

Note why this is important. It prevents us from puffing ourselves up and so be deceived ourselves. How often have we seen judgment wielded as a blunt instrument with no love? Far too often. We do so because it makes us feel better about our own sin. But it leads to self-deception as these verses indicate because you start to feel better about yourself when someone else is in the crosshairs. Have you ever had to deal with the super-spirituals in church? The people who are always in the prominent pew. Pray the loudest. Act the holiest. Fast to be seen. Praise to be heard. Beloved, there are no super-spirituals in the church. Your pastor is just a brother with a different calling than you. We all share the same Spirit, which is from God. We are all sinners, who thanks to the mercy and grace of Almighty God have been forgiven.

---

[20] **Trespass:** (Gr. *paraptōma*) This is a sin that can come in the way of some desire (lusting), some thinking (entertaining a wrongdoing) or some action (carrying out one's desires or thoughts that he or she has been entertaining) that is beyond or overstepping God's righteous standards, as set out in the Scriptures. It is falling or making a false step as opposed to standing or walking upright in harmony with the righteous requirements of God.–Matt. 6:14; Mark 11:25; Rom. 4:25; 5:15-20; 11:11; 2 Cor. 5:19; Gal. 6:1; Eph. 1:7; 2:1, 5; Col 2:13.

So, when it comes to judge not as related to sin, it is not about one being better than another. It is not about our pride. It has to be motivated out of love. It has to be carried out in gentleness. It has to be free from hypocrisy. The judge not verses make it clear that there still is a speck in the eye of your brother and Jesus does not say to leave it there. He always says - go and sin no more. Removing the plank in our own eye first humbles us to realize we are not better than our brother or sister. It forces us to consider the burden they carry, lest we become conceited into a false sense of super-spirituality. We are our brother's keeper. If not now, when? If not us, who?

The other primary reason we misuse "judge not" is when Christians want to defend their favorite false teacher or false prophet. As someone who writes a great deal of discernment devotionals regarding the teaching and abuses within the church, I can tell you that inevitably there are always more reactions defending the person espousing false teaching than there are people defending the purity of the Gospel. One of the most often used defenses is "judge not." As we see however from the Matthew verses, the judge not reference has nothing to do with exposing false teachers whatsoever. Even if it did, we eventually come to verse five where Jesus still says we are to help our brother remove the speck from their eye. To make matters even worse with their biblical illiteracy however we then see the same people accusing those who are standing for the truth as causing division. That is the opposite of what the Bible teaches:

Romans 16:17-18 Updated American Standard Version (UASV)

[17] Now I urge you, brothers, to keep your eye on those who cause divisions and occasions of stumbling contrary to the teaching that you have learned, and turn away from them. [18] For such men are slaves, not of our Lord Christ but of their own appetites; and by their smooth and flattering speech they deceive the hearts of the unsuspecting.

Read these verses carefully beloved. It is not people objecting to false teaching that cause division but doctrine contrary to the true Gospel of Jesus Christ. When you preach a prosperity gospel, you are dividing the body of Christ. When you preach a hyper-grace gospel, you are dividing the body of Christ. When you preach word-faith, bridal paradigm nonsense, false signs and lying wonders, or any other contrary gospel you are dividing the body of Christ. Instead, we see the opposite in the church today. We see a Joel Osteen preach a completely heretical gospel filled with word faith lies, prosperity lies, and false salvation lies and when someone points out the lies the people say - judge not! You don't know his heart! I do not have to know his heart. I only have to discern his teaching. Jesus warns us about this with frightening eternal consequences!

Matthew 7:21-23 Updated American Standard Version (UASV)

²¹ "Not everyone who says to me, 'Lord, Lord,' will enter the kingdom of heaven, but the one who does the will of my Father who is in heaven. ²² On that day many will say to me, 'Lord, Lord, did we not prophesy in your name, and cast out demons in your name, and do many mighty works in your name?' ²³ And then I will declare to them, 'I never knew you; depart from me, you who practice lawlessness.'

Beloved, do we truly understand the gravity of these verses? This is the day we stand before Christ. This is it. No turning back. Our fate decided. Either the blessings of heaven and eternal life await or the burning fires of hell and eternal damnation. This is no game. Take a look at what these people did. They prophesied in His name! They cast out demons and performed mighty works in His name! These are people who obviously thought they were serving God. They certainly thought their sincerity would be enough. They may have felt they served Him their entire life. When they saw the mighty works and signs and wonders they must have felt confirmed that they were on the right path. Yet He says He never even knew them! Depart from me! You can have a church building packed with 50,000 people every week. It does not matter. You can have a respected "prophetic ministry" where you feel you encourage thousands of people at a time. It does not matter. The only thing that matters is if He knows you. If you are found in Him by being in His Word. Not in the word of man. Only in the Word of God. That is the more unbelievable point. In order to truly believe that judge not means we ignore false teaching and prophecy means we have to ignore huge swaths of Scripture:

Colossians 2:8 Updated American Standard Version (UASV)

⁸ See to it that no one takes you captive through philosophy[21] and empty deception, according to the tradition of men, according to the elementary things of the world and not according to Christ.

2 Timothy 4:3-4 Updated American Standard Version (UASV)

³ For there will be a time when they will not put up with sound teaching, but in accordance with their own desires, they will accumulate teachers for themselves to have their ears tickled,[22] ⁴ and will turn away

---

[21] The NIV reads, "See to it that no one takes you captive through hollow and deceptive philosophy" and the NET Bible reads, "Be careful not to allow anyone to captivate you through an empty, deceitful philosophy ..." In other words, there is nothing wrong with philosophy (i.e., love of wisdom), but we should be weary of hollow, deceptive, or empty philosophy.

[22] Or *to tell them what they want to hear*

their ears from the truth and will turn aside to myths. ⁵ But you, be sober-minded²³ in all things, endure hardship, do the work of an evangelist, fulfill your ministry.

Matthew 7:15 Updated American Standard Version (UASV)

¹⁵ "Beware of the false prophets, who come to you in sheep's clothing, but inwardly are ravenous wolves.

Galatians 1:6-9 Updated American Standard Version (UASV)

⁶ I am amazed that you are so quickly deserting him who called you in the grace of Christ and are turning to a different gospel; ⁷ not that there is another, but there are some who trouble you and want to distort the gospel of Christ. ⁸ But even if we or an angel from heaven should proclaim to you a gospel contrary to²⁴ the one we preached to you, let him be accursed!²⁵ ⁹ As we said before, and now I say again, if anyone is proclaiming a gospel to you contrary to²⁶ what you have received, let him be accursed!²⁷

Jude 1:4 Updated American Standard Version (UASV)

⁴ Certain men have crept in among you who were long ago appointed for this judgment, ungodly men²⁸ who turn the grace of our God into an excuse for licentiousness²⁹ and who prove false to our only Master and Lord, Jesus Christ.

1 Timothy 4:1-4 Updated American Standard Version (UASV)

Spirit explicitly says that in later times some will fall away from the faith, paying attention to deceitful spirits and doctrines of demons,

Acts 20:28-30 Updated American Standard Version (UASV)

²⁸ Pay careful attention to yourselves and to all the flock, in which the Holy Spirit has made you overseers, to care for the congregation³⁰ of God, which he obtained with the blood of his own Son.³¹ ²⁹ I know that

---

²³ **Sober Minded:** (Gr. *nepho*) This denotes being sound in mind, to be in control of one's thought processes and thus not be in danger of irrational thinking, 'to be sober-minded, to be well composed in mind.'–1 Thessalonians 5:6, 8; 2 Timothy 4:5; 1 Peter 1:13; 4:7; 5:8
²⁴ Or *other than*
²⁵ Gr *anathema*
²⁶ Or *other than*
²⁷ Gr *anathema*
²⁸ Lit *irreverential (ones)*
²⁹ Or loose conduct; shameless conduct (Gr *aselgeia*) behavior completely lacking in moral restraint, usually with the implication of sexual licentiousness – 'licentious behavior, extreme immorality.'
³⁰ Gr *ekklesia* ("assembly;" "congregation, i.e., of Christians")
³¹ Lit *with the blood of his Own.*

after my departure fierce wolves will come in among you, not sparing the flock; ³⁰ and from among your own selves men will arise, speaking twisted things, to draw away the disciples after them.

2 Peter 2:1-3 Updated American Standard Version (UASV)

2 But false prophets also arose among the people, just as there will also be false teachers among you, who will secretly introduce destructive heresies, even denying the Master who bought them, bringing swift destruction upon themselves. ² Many will follow their acts of shameless conduct,³² and because of them the way of the truth will be spoken of abusively; ³ and in their greed they will exploit you with false words; their judgment from long ago is not idle, and their destruction is not asleep.

2 Timothy 4:3-4 Updated American Standard Version (UASV)

³ For there will be a time when they will not put up with sound teaching, but in accordance with their own desires, they will accumulate teachers for themselves to have their ears tickled,³³ ⁴ and will turn away their ears from the truth and will turn aside to myths. ⁵ But you, be sober-minded³⁴ in all things, endure hardship, do the work of an evangelist, fulfill your ministry.

2 Corinthians 11:13-15 Updated American Standard Version (UASV)

¹³ For such men are false apostles, deceitful workers, disguising themselves as apostles of Christ. ¹⁴ And no wonder, for even Satan disguises himself as an angel of light. ¹⁵ Therefore it is not a great thing if his servants also disguise themselves as servants of righteousness, whose end will be according to their deeds.

Look at this list of Scripture! This is not even a complete listing of the warnings to us about false teaching and prophecy. We are to stand idly by at all. We are not to turn a blind eye with a wink, a nod and a "judge not." Let us consider four more sets of Scriptures related to this:

Titus 1:9 Updated American Standard Version (UASV)

⁹ holding fast to the faithful word which is in accordance with the teaching, so that he will be able both to exhort in sound doctrine and to refute those who contradict.

---

³² Or *their sensuality; their licentious ways; their brazen conduct*
³³ Or *to tell them what they want to hear*
³⁴ **Sober Minded:** (Gr. *nepho*) This denotes being sound in mind, to be in control of one's thought processes and thus not be in danger of irrational thinking, 'to be sober-minded, to be well composed in mind.'–1 Thessalonians 5:6, 8; 2 Timothy 4:5; 1 Peter 1:13; 4:7; 5:8

Acts 17:10-11 Updated American Standard Version (UASV)

10 The brothers immediately sent Paul and Silas away by night to Berea, and when they arrived, they went into the synagogue of the Jews. 11 Now these were more noble-minded than those in Thessalonica, who received the word with all eagerness,[35] examining the Scriptures daily to see whether these things were so.

1 Thessalonians 5:16-22 Updated American Standard Version (UASV)

16 Rejoice always; 17 pray without ceasing; 18 in everything give thanks; for this is God's will for you in Christ Jesus. 19 Do not quench the Spirit; 20 do not treat prophecies as nothing. 21 But examine everything carefully; hold fast to that which is good; 22 abstain from every form of evil.

1 John 4:1 Updated American Standard Version (UASV)

4 Beloved ones, do not believe every spirit, but test the spirits to see whether they are from God, for many false prophets have gone out into the world.

In Titus, he is addressing anyone who would seek a leadership role in the church. Deacons, elders or pastors. Not only must we hold firm to the trustworthy Word as taught but we must be prepared to rebuke those who contradict it! This is not optional beloved. As a minister of the Gospel of Jesus Christ, I am commanded to rebuke those that would preach a different Gospel. I have seen people proclaim we are all on the same team and that is simply not true. If you do not preach the whole Gospel of Jesus Christ, I am not on your team. More importantly, you are not on His. Unity is not a Christian catchphrase. It does not mean we all hold hands and sing Kumbaya while skipping down the broad path that leads to destruction. It means we call a devil a devil and refuse to associate with him.

Also related to sound doctrine, we see the verses from Acts 17, where Paul visited Berea. The Bereans were more noble because they not only received the Word with eagerness, but they checked it against Scripture to make sure what they were being taught was accurate. As previously noted, in the church today we have far too much pastor worship. We are supposed to worship Christ. My pastor always points me back to Christ. That is one of the things that makes him a great pastor. Today in the pews we have some of the eagerness regarding receiving the Word but no Berean spirit actually to check if it is accurate. That is why false doctrine is spreading so fast throughout the body. I saw Joel Osteen recently at Yankee stadium

---

[35] Or with all *readiness of mind*. The Greek word *prothumias* means that one is eager, ready, mentally prepared to engage in some activity.

declare that the Bible says we are to declare that which is not as though it were. Sounded great and fit nicely with his overall heretical word-faith message but there was only one problem:

Romans 4:17 Updated American Standard Version (UASV)

[17] (as it is written, "A father of many nations have I made you") in the presence of Him whom he believed, even God, who gives life to the dead and who calls the things that are not as though they are,

What Osteen stated was simply untrue. This verse he was referring to cannot be clearer. It is GOD who calls what is not as though it were - not us! May seem subtle and harmless except for those who eagerly bought it and now believe something that is untrue. It does not just end there. Osteen does this all the time. So, does Joseph Prince, and nearly every false teacher there is. We must cultivate the Berean spirit within us and stop being so gullible for men who seek to make merchandise of His Word.

The final two sets of verses here deal more specifically with false prophecies - which is also rampant in the church today and defended by a chorus of judge not! The Thessalonians verses spell out for us what the will of God is for our life. We are not to despise prophecy, but in order to get there, we must first test everything! Only then, after careful discernment and using God's Word as our plumb line, can we hold fast to what is good. Beloved, there are more spirits than the Holy Spirit in our realm of spiritual warfare. We fight against rulers of the dark realms and principalities. As the 1John verses teach us, many false prophets are in the world, and we must test the spirits to see if they are indeed from God. This year I was witness to a weekend visitation of a false prophet to a local church. For three nights I observed a mangling of the Word of God along with witchcraft passed off as "prophecy," and the people ate it up. There was no way I was going to allow him to lay hands on me. It was obvious there was no involvement of the Holy Spirit, which meant he was operating in different spirits. Worldly spirits. These are spirits under the dominion of Satan. The Bible says we are to have nothing to do with the works of darkness but rather expose them. It seems like the church has dove off the theological cliff in pursuit of spiritual experiences not realizing that not every spiritual experience is from the Holy Spirit. We must test, discern, and hold onto what is good. What is of God.

So, judge not? Ehh...not so fast. This Christianism is abusing a set of Scriptures that actually teaches the opposite. Don't lose sight of that. Jesus is teaching in those verses that we ARE to judge, only after ensuring we are not being hypocritical. We ARE to help our brother or sister with the speck in their eye. It is to be done with a loving spirit, not a critical spirit. Jesus said they would know us by our love. How can we say we love someone when we think helping them with something that separates them from God is "judgment?" How is it love to say nothing to someone who we know is sitting under false teaching? Teaching that could damage their walk or even lead them astray from God? Or even worse, teaching that could lead them to falsely believe they are saved when they really are not? How is that love? It is not. It is simply cruelty wrapped up in a sentence fragment; whose full context teaches the exact opposite. Christ demands more from us than that.

CHAPTER FOUR The General Tithing Lie

Before we can get into the specific lies used by tithing proponents, we need to lay the groundwork for understanding what tithing was in the Bible. It is not a made-up word nor concept. The word "tithe" literally means 10 percent. Tithing was established within the Mosaic law to ensure the sustainability of the nation of Israel as God designed it. This chapter will have quite a bit of Scripture because it is important to see all God did say about tithing, so we can more easily understand and see how it is being abused today. It is important to make a distinction first between the system of tithing and the mere mention of the word. It is true that the word tithe appears prior to the Mosaic law but in those instances, it was used merely as denoting a tenth of something. When we get into the specific lies, we will explain this further. The problem is that the hucksters of today that are trying to enforce tithing as being a biblical principle are obviously speaking about the system of tithing that God established in the Mosaic law. This will become clearer as we move forward through the lies. Here is the first mention of tithing in the Bible:

Leviticus 27:30-33 Updated American Standard Version (UASV)

30 'Every tenth part[36] of the land, whether of the seed of the land or of the fruit of the trees, belongs to Jehovah. It is something holy to Jehovah 31 If a man wishes to redeem some of his tenth part, he shall add a fifth to it. 32 For every tenth part of herd or flock, whatever passes under the rod, the tenth one[37] shall be holy to Jehovah. 33 He is not to be concerned whether it is good or bad, nor shall he exchange it; or if he does exchange it, then both it and its substitute shall become holy. It shall not be redeemed.'"

Again, please note that this is the first mention of the system of tithing, not the mere usage of the word. The snake oil salesmen of today try to muddy the waters to confuse people, but they are trying to sell the notion that God established a system of tithing that remains in effect today. That goes back to the establishment of tithing as a system, not simply using the word to describe a tenth of something. The introduction here serves as a reminder to Israel that they are in effect tenants upon the land which God has given them. The forced system of tithing reminds them who is

---

[36] Or *Every tithe*
[37] Lit *tenth head*

responsible for their increase. The initial answer from the pro-tithing crowd would be in favor of continuing this practice. I agree. I think it is always good and right to remember that it is the Lord that provides. That does not mean however that we are bound by this system as it is enforced by many today. That is the larger point. The New Testament makes clear the new guidelines for giving that do not include tithing as a forced system. What I want us to take out from this first set of verses, however, is what the tithe is comprised of. Seed of the land, fruit of the trees, and herds and flocks. No mention of money whatsoever. Wait a minute preacher! Israel was an agrarian society, so it is only logical that they would tithe from produce, but we now have money! That lie won't stand either because the Israelites had money too:

Exodus 30:11-16 Updated American Standard Version (UASV)

¹¹ Jehovah also spoke to Moses, saying, ¹² "When you take the sum of the sons of Israel to number them, then each one of them shall give a ransom for his soul to Jehovah, when you number them, so that there will be no plague among them when you number them. ¹³ Each one who is numbered in the census shall give this: half a shekel according to the shekel of the sanctuary (the shekel[38] is twenty gerahs), half a shekel as an offering to Jehovah. ¹⁴ Everyone who is numbered, from twenty years old and over, shall give the offering of Jehovah. ¹⁵ The rich shall not give more, and the poor shall not give less, than the half shekel, when they give the offering of Jehovah, to make atonement for your souls. ¹⁶ You shall take the atonement money from the sons of Israel and shall give it for the service of the tent of meeting, that it may bring the sons of Israel to remembrance before Jehovah, so as to make atonement for your souls."

The Bible tells us of two occurrences prior to the setting up of the Mosaic Law in which ten percent of one's possessions was paid to God or to one of his representatives. The first occasion was when Abraham gave Melchizedek a tenth of everything of his victory over Chedorlaomer and his allies. (Gen. 14:18-20) The second occasion concerned Jacob, who

---

[38] **Stumble, fall away, to be offended:** (Gr. *skandalizomai*) In Greek, "stumbling block" (*skandalon*) was originally a device or trap, which contained bait, to ensnare or catch something alive. (1 John 2:10) It is used in the Scriptures as a trap, obstacle, or snare that stumbles one into sinning. (Rom. 11:9; Matt. 13:41) It can also be used as an obstacle that causes offense, resulting in opposition. (1 Cor. 1:23; Gal. 5:11) The Greek, (*skandalizomai*) refers to one who ceases to believe because of tribulation. (Matt. 13:21) It can also refer to one who is spiritually weak, immature in the faith, resulting in their falling into sin. (2 Cor. 11:29) In addition, it can refer to one who takes offense to some action. (Matt. 15:12) It can refer to one who causes another no longer to believe (John 6:61) It can also refer to something or someone that causes another to sin because they are spiritually weak or immature in the faith. (Matt. 5:29; Rom. 14:21) It can refer to another who is angered or shocked by something or someone, which could result in their sinning. – Matt. 17:27; John 6:61.

vowed at Bethel to "give a full tenth" of his substance to God. (Gen. 28:20-22) As early as the days of Abraham, precious metals such as gold and silver served as money. The book of Job was penned about 1473 B.C.E.[39] Abraham was born about 2018 B.C.E. and died about 1843 B.C.E., 370 years before the book of Job. The time covered in the book of Job was over 140 years between 1657 and 1473 B.C.E. Money is mentioned there as well:

Job 42:10-11 Updated American Standard Version (UASV)

10 And Jehovah restored the fortunes of Job, when he had prayed for his friends. And the Lord gave Job twice as much as he had before. 11 Then all his brothers and all his sisters and all who had known him before came to him, and they ate bread with him in his house; and they consoled him and comforted him for all the adversities that Jehovah had brought on him. And each one gave him one piece of money,[40] and each a ring of gold.

The overall point here is that tithing was never designed to involve money. The adaptation of an agrarian system to the modern method of fleecing the flock is not only clever but the sleight of hand used with Scripture is treacherous. We continue with the examination of tithing as it was established within the Mosaic Law.

Numbers 18:21-32 Updated American Standard Version (UASV)

21 "To the sons of Levi, behold, every tenth part[41] in Israel as an inheritance in return for the service they are carrying out, the service of the tent of meeting. 22 The sons of Israel shall not come near the tent of meeting again, or they will bear sin and die. 23 Only the Levites shall perform the service of the tent of meeting, and they shall bear their iniquity; it shall be a perpetual statute throughout your generations, and among the sons of Israel they shall have no inheritance. 24 For the tenth part of the sons of Israel, which they offer as an offering to Jehovah, I have given to the Levites for an inheritance; therefore I have said concerning them, 'They shall have no inheritance among the sons of Israel.'"

25 Then Jehovah spoke to Moses, saying, 26 "Moreover, you shall speak to the Levites and say to them, 'When you take from the sons of

---

[39] B.C.E. means "before the Common Era," which is more accurate than B.C. ("before Christ"). C.E. denotes "Common Era," often called A.D., for *anno Domini*, meaning "in the year of our Lord." Note that time moved forward by going down during the B.C.E. years, while time moved forward by going up during the C.E. years.
[40] Lit *gave him one qesitah*. A unit of money with no known value.
[41] Or *the tithe*

Israel the tithe which I have given you from them for your inheritance, then you shall present an offering from it to Jehovah, a tenth part of the tenth part. ²⁷ Your offering shall be reckoned to you as the grain from the threshing floor or the full produce from the winepress. ²⁸ So you shall also present an offering to Jehovah from your tenth parts, which you receive from the sons of Israel; and from it you shall give Jehovah's offering to Aaron the priest. ²⁹ Out of all your gifts you shall present every offering due to Jehovah, from all the best of them, ⁴² its sacred part from them.' ³⁰ You shall say to them, 'When you have offered⁴³ from it the best of it, then the rest shall be reckoned to the Levites as the product of the threshing floor, and as the product of the winepress. ³¹ You may eat it anywhere, you and your household, because it is a wage in return for your service in the tent of meeting. ³² You will bear no sin by reason of it when you have offered⁴⁴ the best of it.⁴⁵ But you shall not profane the sacred gifts of the sons of Israel, or you will die.'"

Without getting to technical in the inner workings of Israel, we can see here some relevant truths to capture when we seek to understand tithing. Israel consisted of certain tribes, which were descendent from the sons of Jacob. For example, one of Jacob's sons was named Judah and Jesus lineage can be traced back through the tribe of Judah. This is why He is also known as the Lion of the Tribe of Judah. Another one of the sons of Jacob was named Levi and thus the descendants with his tribe were known as the Levites. They were chosen to be the priests for the people of Israel because they were the only tribe that did not worship the golden calf in Exodus 32. When it came time to divide the Promised Land between the tribes, we see that Levi did not get a portion:

Joshua 18:7 Updated American Standard Version (UASV)

⁷ The Levites have no portion among you, for the priesthood of Jehovah is their inheritance. And Gad and Reuben and half the tribe of Manasseh have received their inheritance beyond the Jordan eastward, which Moses the servant of Jehovah gave them."

Even though they had no designated land, the other tribes allotted them cities, in which to live and they served the religious needs of the nation. We see from these verses in the Book of Numbers that those duties included ensuring that the other tribes did not come near the Tent of Meeting, lest they die for their sins. Because the Levites work was consecrated unto the Lord and they had no real land to call their own, they

---

⁴² Lit *fat*
⁴³ Lit *lifted*
⁴⁴ Lit *lifted*
⁴⁵ Lit *fat*

did not work the land and thus needed to be provided for. Enter the tithing system. We see from these verses that their inheritance was the tithe from the other tribes. The Levites were also commanded to tithe to God from the tithes they received so as not to profane the holy things of the people of Israel.

This is where the sleight of hand takes place. The logic employed by the pro-tithing crowd is as follows. The Levites performed the religious work of the Lord and were supported by the people of the Lord with ten percent off the top of everything they made. Today, the pastors are the Levites. They perform the religious work of the Lord and should be supported by the people of the Lord with the same ten percent system He already established. That sounds great, but there are some glaring problems. First of all, as already established, the tithe was never money even though money existed. The reason tithing was set up is God decreed that the Levites were not to work. He has made no such decree regarding pastors in the New Testament church. We all know that the Apostle Paul maintained his occupation as a tentmaker for example. This is not to say that a pastor is forbidden from drawing a salary for administering a church. Watch the sleight of hand here. You can make a cogent scriptural argument for paying pastors, but you cannot use the agrarian tithing system as the defense. Remember, no one is suggesting the people of God should not give to the work of God. The lie is in demanding it as a forced system called tithing, which is completely unbiblical for New Testament believers. What's the big deal? Tithing is nothing more than abusing the sheep of God. It is wielded like a hammer over God's people. By insisting that it is a system established by God for today you accuse people of being disobedient to God if they do not tithe. I have seen pastor-hustlers tell their sheep that the reason they are not conceiving a child is because they are not tithing correctly. Or the reason they lost their job. Or the reason someone in their family died. The depravity knows no end for those who do not truly fear the Lord. We have two more sets of Scriptures regarding tithing as established in the Mosaic Law.

Deuteronomy 14:22-29 Updated American Standard Version (UASV)

[22] "You shall surely a tenth[46] all the produce from your seed,[47] which comes out of the field every year. [23] You shall eat in the presence of Jehovah your God, at the place where he chooses to make his name dwell there, the tenth part of your grain, your new wine, your oil, and the firstborn of your herd and your flock, so that you may learn to fear Jehovah

---

[46] Or *a tithe*
[47] Or *what you sow*

your God always. ²⁴ And if the way is too long for you, so that you are not able to carry the tenth part, since the place where Jehovah your God chooses to set his name is too far away from you when Jehovah your God blesses you, ²⁵ then you shall turn it into money and bind up the money in your hand and go to the place that the Lord your God chooses. ²⁶ You may spend the money for whatever your soul[48] desires: for oxen, or sheep, or wine, or strong drink, or whatever your soul asks of you;[49] and there you shall eat in the presence of Jehovah your God and rejoice, you and your household. ²⁷ And the Levite that is within your gates, you shall not forsake him; for he has no portion or inheritance among you.

²⁸ "At the end of every three years you shall bring forth all the tenth part of your produce in the same year, and shall lay it up within your gates. ²⁹ And the Levite, because he has no portion or inheritance among you, and the sojourner, and the fatherless, and the widow, that are within your gates, shall come, and shall eat and be satisfied; in order that Jehovah your God may bless you in all the work of your hand which you do.

There are some differing opinions about whether this is an additional tithe required by the Lord or merely more in-depth instructions. It matters not for this discussion because it only reinforces what we have already discussed. Even though money is mentioned it is only related to not being able to carry the tithe. The care for the Levites is referenced again, but again, the system set up had them incapable of producing their own food. What is also interesting here is we see the heart of the Lord. Caring about the sojourner, the fatherless and the widow. This theme is consistent throughout the Bible:

James 1:27 Updated American Standard Version (UASV)

²⁷ Pure and undefiled religion before[50] our God and Father is this: to visit orphans and widows in their affliction, and to keep oneself unstained by the world.

I point this out because the modern tithing system has hijacked this basic principle from God. I have heard local pastors tell their congregations that they cannot spend their tithe on helping other Christians in need. Cannot spend it on helping the fatherless, the widow or the orphan. That if you choose to sow into this or that ministry instead, then don't bother asking me to visit you in the hospital. I am not joking. I heard this from the pulpit. I have heard national preachers claim you curse all of your money if you don't tithe to them. The interesting thing then is that many preachers will refuse to reveal how they spent your tithe. I have heard preachers claim that it is none of your business what they do with it. God did not institute

---

[48] Or *heart*
[49] Or *desires*
[50] Or *in the sight of*

such a system. He wants everyone to come, eat and be filled just as His desire is for all to come to repentance. These verses from Deuteronomy 14 reveal the heart of God and only the wicked heart of man can take something so good and turn it on its head like is done with the modern tithing system. Only the wicked heart of man can demand that you turn a blind eye to need and blame it on God. The last set of verses regarding tithing in the Mosaic Law is found in Deuteronomy chapter 26:

Deuteronomy 26:1-19 Updated American Standard Version (UASV)

26 "And it shall be, when you come into the land that Jehovah your God gives you as an inheritance, and you possess it and live in it, 2 that you shall take of the first of all the fruit of the ground, which you shall bring in from your land that Jehovah your God gives you; and you shall put it in a basket, and shall go to the place where Jehovah your God shall choose, to make his name to dwell there. 3 And you shall come to the priest who is in office in those days, and say to him, 'I declare this day to Jehovah your God, that I have entered the land which Jehovah swore to our fathers to give us. 4 Then the priest shall take the basket from your hand and set it down before the altar of Jehovah your God. 5 "And you shall make response before Jehovah your God, 'A wandering Aramean[51] was my father. And he went down into Egypt and sojourned there, few in number, and there he became a nation, great, mighty, and populous. 6 And the Egyptians treated us harshly and afflicted us and laid on us hard labor. 7 Then we cried to Jehovah, the God of our fathers, and Jehovah heard our voice and saw our affliction, our toil, and our oppression; 8 and Jehovah brought us out of Egypt with a mighty hand and an outstretched arm and with great terror and with signs and wonders; 9 and he has brought us to this place and has given us this land, a land flowing with milk and honey. 10 Now behold, I have brought the first of the produce of the ground which you, O Jehovah have given me.' And you shall set it down before Jehovah your God, and worship before Jehovah your God; 11 and you shall rejoice in all the good that the Lord your God has given to you

---

[51] **Aram; Aramaeans:** (Heb. *arămmi*) These were the descendants of Shem's son Aram, who mainly lived in various regions N of Israel, running from the Lebanon Mountains across to Mesopotamia and from the Taurus Mountains in the north down to Damascus. The Aramaeans hardly ever formed any kind of nation state; rather they lived as self-governing, autonomous towns and tribes settled by nomads before 1000 B.C.E. However, if they were threatened, they were quick to form alliances with neighboring towns of Aramaeans and even other countries. However, once the threat was over, they went back to their independence, fighting amongst themselves. The area known as Aram in Hebrew would later be referred to as Syria, and its people as the Syrians. – Gen. 25:20; Deut. 26:5; Hos 12:12.

FLEECING THE FLOCK

and to your house, you, and the Levite, and the foreign resident who is among you.

¹² "When you finish tithing the entire tenth of your produce in the third year, the year of the tenth, you will give it to the Levite, the foreign resident, the fatherless boy, and the widow, and they will eat their fill within your gates. ¹³ You shall say before Jehovah your God, 'I have removed the sacred portion from my house, and also have given it to the Levite and the foreign resident, the fatherless and the widow, according to all your commandments which you have commanded me; I have not transgressed or forgotten any of your commandments. ¹⁴ I have not eaten of it while mourning, nor have I removed any of it while I was unclean, nor offered any of it to the dead. I have listened to the voice of Jehovah my God; I have done according to all that you have commanded me. ¹⁵ Look down from your holy habitation, from heaven, and bless your people Israel, and the ground which you have given us, as you swore to our fathers, a land flowing with milk and honey.'

¹⁶ "This day Jehovah your God commands you to do these statutes and ordinances. You shall, therefore, be careful to do them with all your heart and with all your soul. ¹⁷ You have declared today that Jehovah is your God, and that you would walk in his ways and keep his statutes, his commandments and his ordinances, and listen to his voice. ¹⁸ And Jehovah has declared today that you are a people for his treasured possession, as he has promised you, and that you are to keep all his commandments; ¹⁹ and that he will set you[52] high above all nations which he has made, for praise, fame, and honor; and that you shall be a holy[53] people to Jehovah your God, as he has spoken."

This is actually the entire chapter. A reminder to Israel of what God has brought them through and that He alone is responsible for their increase. We as Christians should celebrate the same concept. We should pay into the work of the kingdom. We should take up the cause of the needy. Neither this book nor my heart declares otherwise. Let us not lose sight however of what this chapter is. It is one of the closing chapters in the Torah. It is part of the Mosaic Law. It is important to distinguish the three portions of the Mosaic Law. The first is the Moral Law. These laws are said to be based on the character of God. They are presented for the benefit of those who would follow it. This is a crucial understanding missed by the likes of Joseph Prince and the lawless antinomian crowd. To them, the law is always a bad thing, but the reality is the law is for our benefit. Consider them like guardrails on the highway we call life. Without them, we can

---

[52] Lit *and to set you*
[53] Or *consecrated*; pertaining to what is dedicated in service to God

drive ourselves right off a cliff! The second set is known as the Ceremonial Law. These are customs set up specifically for the Nation of Israel and were not meant to be carried forward. These are the laws that drive unbelievers crazy because they do not understand them. Why was it forbidden to eat shellfish for example? We see in society today the purposeful mixing of these branches of law to confuse the issue on sin. When defending homosexuality for example, the refrain is always that if we follow that law, then we shouldn't eat shellfish either because that too is called an abomination. Of course, the sin of homosexuality is part of the moral code while the admonition against shellfish was part of the ceremonial law. Jesus also clarifies this in the New Testament:

Acts 10:9-16 Updated American Standard Version (UASV)

⁹ The next day, as they were on their journey and approaching the city, Peter went up on the housetop about the sixth hour[54] to pray. ¹⁰ But he became hungry and was desiring to eat; but while they were making preparations, he fell into a trance; ¹¹ and he saw the heavens opened and something like a great sheet descending, being let down by its four corners upon the earth, ¹² and in it were all sorts of four-footed animals and reptiles[55] of the earth and birds of heaven. ¹³ And there came a voice to him: "Rise, Peter; kill and eat." ¹⁴ But Peter said, "By no means, Lord; for I have never eaten anything that is common or unclean." ¹⁵ And the voice came to him again a second time, "What God has made clean, do not call common." ¹⁶ And this happened three times, and immediately the object[56] was taken up into heaven.

God understands our propensity to get things easily confused. Peter was still holding on to the dietary codes written in the Ceremonial Law. God had to correct him and show him that now, he was no longer to call what God has made unclean. We will see the same concept when it comes to tithing, but tithing was part of the third branch, the Civil Law. These revolve around the civil organization of the nation. Tithing proponents will argue there is a moral imperative to tithing but one cannot ignore that the primary function was that of a tax for the purpose of maintaining the Tribe of Levi. It was entirely civil in nature.

We are not the nation of Israel, despite the movement within Christianity that turns Israel into an idol. Israel was set up as a theocracy, with God as their King. Eventually, they demanded an earthly king but a theocracy it remained. We do not live in a theocracy, despite many in

---

[54] I.e., about 12:00 noon.
[55] Or *crawling creatures*
[56] Lit *vessel*

Christianity who seem to think we should. We are not bound by rules and regulations that were designed to moderate the nation of Israel. The moral rules, however, were carried forward and reaffirmed in the New Testament:

Romans 13:8-10 Updated American Standard Version (UASV)

[8] Owe nothing to anyone, except to love one another, for the one who loves someone else has fulfilled the law. [9] For the commandments, "You shall not commit adultery, you shall not commit murder, you shall not steal, you shall not covet,"[57] and if there is any other commandment, are summed up in this statement: "You shall love your neighbor as yourself."[58] [10] Love does not work evil to a neighbor; therefore love is the fulfilling of the law.

Galatians 5:14 Updated American Standard Version (UASV)

[14] For the whole law is fulfilled in one word: "You shall love your neighbor as yourself."

Galatians 6:2 Updated American Standard Version (UASV)

[2] Bear one another's burdens, and so fulfill the law of Christ.

We can see from these three verse sets that God is not talking about how to muzzle your ox or the ceremonial uncleanness of certain animals. This is a moral imperative to love one another, not a ceremonial or civil instruction.

Tithing is a biblical word beloved. It literally means tenth in Hebrew. Tithing, however, was a system set up by God to manage the theocracy of Israel civilly. To ensure that the Tribe of Levi was sustained and to remind the people who their source is. Today as Christians we have the same source, and we too should never forget that. But to pretend that means we are to adhere to a 3000-year-old agrarian system by turning over 10% of our income to the local preacher or church is simply ridiculous on its face. Like with the dietary laws however God does not leave us to our own devices. He has clearly spelled out for us in the New Testament how giving is supposed to be handled.

---

[57] A quotation from Ex. 20:13-15, 17; Deut. 5:17-19, 21
[58] A quotation from Lev. 19:18

Anthony Wade

CHAPTER FIVE The Malachi Lies

There is perhaps no Bible book more abused than the poor Prophet Malachi. Specifically, Malachi Chapter Three. Modern churchgoers know it well. Possibly as well as John 3:16. That is because nearly every time a pastor wants to take an offering they refer to Malachi Chapter Three. The problem is that they rip the verses horribly out of context and seemingly have never bothered to exposit the rest of the book at all. This goes for good pastors and false alike. It is how they were taught. In order to fully understand Malachi Chapter Three, we will look at the entire book. Remember that originally there were no chapters in the original texts. The chapters and verses we see today were not added until the 13th Century C.E. So, when Malachi wrote his book it was one book, not four chapters. So, to properly understand the full context, we start at the beginning.

Malachi was a prophet living somewhere during the time of Ezra and Nehemiah. This is during the time that the remnant returned to Jerusalem after the captivity in Babylon. While short in length, Malachi is one of the most frequently cited books in modern churchianity because of his reference to tithing in the third chapter. The result is that Malachi Chapter Three is one of the least understood books in all of the Bible. As we read through the proper context, we will discover there are many direct correlations for the would-be preachers of today that have little to do with tithing and everything to do with a loss of the reverent fear of God from leadership.

Malachi 1:6-8 Updated American Standard Version (UASV)

6 "A son honors his father, and a servant his master. If then I am a father, where is my honor? And if I am a master, where is my fear? says Jehovah of armies[59] to you, O priests, who despise my name. But you say, 'How have we despised your name?' 7 You are presenting defiled bread[60] upon my altar. But you say, 'How have we defiled you?' In that you say, 'The table of Jehovah is to be despised.' 8 When you offer blind animals in sacrifice, is that not evil? And when you offer those that are lame or sick, is

---

[59] **Jehovah of armies:** (Heb. *jhvh tsaba*) literally means an army of soldiers, or military forces (Gen. 21:22; Deut. 20:9). It can also be used figuratively, "the sun and the moon and the stars, all the armies of heaven." (Deut. 4:19) In the plural form, it is also used of the Israelites forces as well. (Ex. 6:26; 7:4; Num. 33:1; Psa. 44:9) However, the "armies" in the expression "Jehovah of armies" is a reference to the angelic forces primarily, if not exclusively.
[60] Or *food*

that not evil? Present that to your governor; will he accept you or show you favor? says Jehovah of armies.

The book opens up with God speaking directly to the priests that rule in Israel. Not the people - the priests. This is vitally important because at no point in the book does the narration change. At no point does the Lord switch and start talking to anyone other than the priests. This dialogue motif remains constant throughout the entire book. God is talking to the priests and the priests responding in doubtful disbelief at their own sins. These were the people who were in charge of the spiritual leadership of God's people. Note the sad statement God has to make here. If I am the Father - where is my honor? If I am the Master - then where is my fear? The implication is quite clear. Those that would claim the mantle of following God should honor and fear Him. More importantly, those in charge of the spiritual leadership of His people should all the more honor and fear Him. Taking a glance along the landscape of modern Christianity today we do not see leadership that operates with honor or fear of the Lord. We simply do not. We see a church that has been willing to compromise the true Gospel of Jesus Christ over and over again. A church that is more concerned with being hip and relevant to a dying world than they are with bringing the world the only way out, Jesus Christ. Too harsh you say? Consider these real events from recent history. How does a "pastor" lead his church by serving iced tea and skittles as the elements of Holy Communion? How does a pastor of thousands invent things like "transportation blessings" to bilk his congregants out of their money to fix his helicopter? How does the most famous pastor in the country, with 45,000 attendees each week, consistently teach self-help instead of God help? Read these opening verses carefully beloved. Sometimes I have people ask me what the big deal is. These verses explain that these people actually despise the name of the Lord! It seems like a big deal to Him! How have we despised your name they ask? By offering polluted food upon my altar.

Matthew 4:4 Updated American Standard Version (UASV)

4 But he answered, "It is written,

"'Man shall not live by bread alone, but by every word that proceeds out of the mouth of God.'"[61]

Food is used constantly throughout Scripture as a metaphor for the Word of God. When we are first saved we are said to build our strength on the milk of the Word before moving onto the deeper "meat" contained in God's Word. Jesus referred to Himself as the Bread of Life. When a pastor speaks in the church, he is indeed feeding the people of God, if his

---

[61] A quotation from Deut. 8:3

exposition is what the authors meant as opposed to his reading his beliefs or views into the text. He is indeed making a sacrificial offering to God. In the Old Testament, the only way to atone for sins was through the sacrificial offering system God had set up. Under the new covenant, however, Jesus Christ took the place of this system as the Lamb of God, the final atonement made for our sins. So instead of offering an animal for sacrifice, the preacher is offering the new covenant. He is offering the only thing that can cover our sins. He is offering the Gospel of Jesus Christ.

But what do we see being offered instead? It is polluted food upon the altar of God. According to God, the priests were offering blind animals for sacrifice. A blind gospel will not lead to Jesus. The Prosperity gospel being preached in far too many churches today is a blind gospel because it does not lead people to Jesus. The people who sit under it have a distorted and inaccurate view of who God is. They think of God as a spiritual ATM. They combine this with the new "friend of God" theologies and poor man-centered worship music, and the result is they serve a god who does not exist. They serve themselves. They serve their own bellies. Man has been recreating God in his own image since the dawn of time but only now have we perfected it.

These opening verses from Malachi also see God saying that lame or sick animals are being offered for sacrifice. We must realize that the sacrificial system was crucial in the old covenant. The Gospel today is crucial for the new covenant. Without truly understanding our place as a sinner before a holy God and our need for a Savior in His Son - we are not saved.

Romans 1:16 Updated American Standard Version (UASV)

[16] For I am not ashamed of the gospel, for it is the power of God for salvation to everyone who believes, to the Jew first and also to the Greek.

You are not saved by a sick Gospel that sacrifices Christ in order to be more seeker friendly. You are not saved by a sick purpose driven church. You are not saved by a sick or lame gospel that talks more about social relevance than it does personal responsibility. You are not saved by a sick gospel that over-emphasizes grace and avoids dealing with the cold hard fact that we are sinners in the hands of a wrathful God. We continue opening chapter over Malachi.

Malachi 1:11-12 Updated American Standard Version (UASV)

[11] For from the rising of the sun to its setting my name will be great among the nations, and in every place incense will be offered to my name, and a pure offering. For my name will be great among the nations, says

Jehovah of armies. ¹² "But you are profaning it by saying, 'The table of Jehovah is polluted, and its fruit, its food, is to be despised.'

The world sees the pitiful antics on TBN and the Church Channel. They see these snake oil salesmen for what they are even when those who claim the mantle of Christ are being duped. When they bring forth their blind, lame, or sickly gospel, they are actually profaning the name of the Lord! Those who sit under it also profane the name of the Lord. Those who turn a blind eye to it when they know better also profane the name of the Lord. The real food of the Lord becomes despised because of it. Many people do not want to hear the true Gospel because all they have seen is the false. The damage is real. Here is the conclusion of Chapter One of the Book of Malachi:

Malachi 1:13-14 Updated American Standard Version (UASV)

¹³ You also say, 'Look, how tiresome!' and you sniff scornfully at it," says Jehovah of armies. "And you bring stolen, lame, and sick animals.[62] Yes, you bring such things as a gift! Should I accept it from your hand?" says Jehovah. ¹⁴ "Cursed is the cunning one who has a male in his flock, but he makes a vow and sacrifices a blemished one to Jehovah. For I am a great King," says Jehovah of armies, "and my name will be feared among the nations."

Isn't this what is happening today when someone has the temerity to call out false teaching for what it is? They snort at it and say - what weariness is this? You're too serious! You're too legalistic! You're sowing disunity! Away with your weariness! Away with your sound doctrine! We have money to make here; in the name of Jesus of course!

And it doesn't matter if that name is profaned because of what they do. If you bring the Word of God in any form at all, I would take serious note of these concluding Words, which came from God directly to those in charge of the spiritual leadership of His people. Cursed be the cheat who has the real Gospel, swears by it, and yet compromises it in what they bring to the people. Think long and hard about that. This is not innocent. You see it is far easier to bring the sick and lame gospel. It is far easier to bring the blind gospel. These are the folks with the big mansions and cable TV deals. These are the ones who are deified by their flock. That is why God calls them a cheat, because they know better. They know the true Gospel offends and they have chosen the path of least resistance. Who cares who actually gets saved? Who cares if there is polluted food on the altar of God?

---

[62] Defective animals were brought to the altar by the priests who had no regard for their sacrificial duties.

Who cares if the name of the Lord is profaned? God cares. You better believe that. We move on to chapter two.

Malachi 2:4-8 Updated American Standard Version (UASV)

4 Then you will know that I have sent this command to you, that my covenant with Levi may stand, says Jehovah of armies. 5 My covenant with him was one of life and peace, and I gave them to him. It was a covenant of fear,[63] and he feared me and stood in awe of my name. 6 True instruction was in his mouth and unrighteousness was not found on his lips; he walked with Me in peace and uprightness, and he turned many back from error.[64] 7 For the lips of a priest should preserve knowledge, and men should seek instruction from his mouth; for he is the messenger of Jehovah of armies. 8 But as for you, you have turned aside from the way; you have caused many to stumble by the instruction; you have corrupted the covenant of Levi," says Jehovah of armies.

As we can see this narrative is still targeted to the Levitical Priests of the time, who were engaging in all sorts of corruption and evil practices. We see the correlation between these priests, who were responsible for the spiritual well-being of God's people, and the would-be preachers of today who are responsible for the same. Chapter Two only delves deeper into what was wrong then and remains wrong today. It opens here with God directly addressing the priests. There is no other interpretation. We will continue to see that the address never changes direction. There is no point in which God has ceased addressing the priests. This will become crucial when reviewing the next chapter. Chapter Two, however, contains two distinct portions that very much apply to Christian leaders today. The first portion we already see deals with the violation of the covenant of Levi and the latter portion deals with the subject of marriage and divorce.

One of the lesser known covenants, the covenant with Levi was actually made with the descendants of Levi, Aaron and his brethren - four generations removed from Levi himself. Exempt from war, the Levites were

---

[63] I.e. *respect; reverence*
[64] **Error**: (Heb., 'āwōn; Gr. *anomia, paranomia*) The Hebrew word *awon* essentially relates to erring, acting illegally or wrongly. This aspect of sin refers to committing a perverseness, wrongness, lawlessness, law breaking, which can also include the rejection of the sovereignty of God. It also focuses on the liability or guilt of one's wicked, wrongful act. This error may be deliberate or accidental; either willful deviation of what is right or unknowingly making a mistake. (Lev. 4:13-35; 5:1-6, 14-19; Num. 15:22-29; Ps 19:12-13) Of course, if it is intentional; then, the consequence is far more serious. (Num. 15:30-31) Error is in opposition to the truth, and those willfully sinning corrupt the truth, a course that only brings forth flagrant sin. (Isa 5:18-23) We can be hardened by the deceitfulness of sin. – Ex 9:27, 34-35; Heb. 3:13-15.

responsible for the spiritual well-being of the people of God. They taught and read the law to the people and assisted with resolving domestic issues amongst them. Let us examine the above verses and apply them to the leaders we see today in the church. The covenant of Levi is supposed to be one of life and peace with fear and awe of God and His name. Do we see this active today in the works of those who stand in the pulpits? No, we do not. There is a rapid erosion of the fear of God throughout this land, and it starts with the leadership. How else do you explain the brashness you see on would be Christian television? They are misusing Scriptures to try and steal money from people. How else can you explain something like the reality television show, "The Preachers of L.A." I have seen the most abhorrent abuse of Scripture from the wolves standing in pulpits today. There is no fear of God and no regard for His name. These six millionaire pastors are only a microcosm of the problem. They are the "low hanging fruit" in that they should be obvious to those who can discern. The sad reality is that the fear of God is no longer taught to up and coming pastors. The purpose driven-seeker friendly models of church growth do not focus on such things. Instead, there is a carnal method of growing man-centered churches. Look at the proper role for preacher pastors listed here in the key verses. They are to have true instruction in their mouths, walk uprightly, and turn people from their sins. Instead today we see the truth routinely compromised, pastors constantly falling from grace, and a gospel-focused not on sin and repentance but rather on a distorted view of grace and earthly prosperity. The truth is that we rarely turn people from their sins anymore. It simply doesn't sell well. Even the poorly theological sinner's prayer has become a microwaved version of its former self, devoid of the need of repentance and filled instead with non-biblical vagueness about inviting Jesus into your heart. According to the key verses, Pastors and preachers are supposed to guard knowledge!

1 Timothy 4:16 Updated American Standard Version (UASV)

[16] Pay close attention to yourself and to your teaching; persevere in these things, for as you do this you will ensure salvation both for yourself and for those who hear you.

You will save yourself and your hearers! This is Paul instructing Timothy! These Malachi 2 verses explain that people should come seeking instruction from the mouths of pastors and preachers. They should have trust in what they are being told. Sadly, many do not check the veracity of what they hear. Hundreds of thousands attend megachurches espousing false doctrine across this land. Hundreds of thousands of goats who are being told they are sheep. Hundreds of thousands who believed the man in the pulpit blindly and instead of being turned from their iniquity they now are deeper in it than ever. Still in darkness but being told they are light. The Bible teaches that type of darkness is the worst.

Matthew 6:22-23 Updated American Standard Version (UASV)

[22] "The eye is the lamp of the body; so then if your eye is simple,[65] your whole body will be full of light. [23] But if your eye is evil,[66] your whole body will be full of darkness. If then the light that is in you is darkness, how great is the darkness!

Consider for a moment how frightening these verses should be. To be duped into thinking our darkness is really light! Have you ever tried to have a conversation with someone sitting under false teaching? If you have then you appreciate these verses more. They are convinced they enjoy the light and it doesn't matter what Scriptures you show them.

Beloved, these leaders have turned aside from God and through their false instruction have caused many to stumble. It was true in the days of Malachi, and it is true today. The true word of God sets captives free and restores sight to the blind. The false gospel however shackles people in their iniquity, causes them to stumble all the more and blinds them from the real truth. When Jesus looked out on the multitudes, He had compassion for them for they were like sheep without a shepherd. The only thing worse though is having a shepherd who isn't in the shepherding business for the sheep but rather for themselves: a shepherd who has no reverent fear of God or His name. A shepherd who uses the Word of God for his own advantage instead of for the good of his hearers. A shepherd who corrupts the covenant of Levi instead of living a life of peace, with true instruction found on his lips, walking in uprightness and trying to turn people from their iniquity. Beware of those who would violate the covenant of Levi.

While the beginning of Chapter Two dealt with the priests violating the covenant of Levi, the end of the chapter deals directly and frankly with the topic of faithlessness in marriage. The world shuns commitment. They actually are starting to consider divorce as enlightenment. People enter marriage knowing it is not a big deal in society if it doesn't work out. There are websites designed specifically to help people have affairs. Unfortunately, when the world looks into the church, they do not see much of a difference. They see Christians employ the same worldly logic and faithlessness when dealing with their own marriages. We have snuffed out the light of the shining city on a hill when it comes to marriage and faith. It is difficult sometimes to blame the masses when all they see from

---

[65] I.e., *clear, sound, sincere, open, focused on good*
[66] Or *bad, wicked*; i.e., *envious*

leadership is more of the same. We have some pastors on their second and third marriages themselves. Pastors constantly being caught in adultery, prostitution or homosexuality. Excuses made from the pulpit but what is the damage to those who follow? Continuing in chapter two we see God make these points to the leaders through His prophet:

Malachi 2:13-16 Updated American Standard Version (UASV)

¹³ This is another thing you do: you are covering Jehovah's altar with tears, with weeping and groaning, because he no longer regards the offering or accepts it with favor from your hand. ¹⁴ And you say, "For what reason?" Because Jehovah has been a witness between you and the wife of your youth, against whom you have dealt treacherously, though she is your companion and your wife by covenant. ¹⁵ But there was one who did not do it, who has a remnant of the spirit. And what was that one seeking? The seed[67] of God. So guard yourselves as to your spirit, and do not deal treacherously with the wife of your youth. ¹⁶ For I hate[68] divorce,"[69] says Jehovah the God of Israel, "and the one who covers his garment with violence," says Jehovah of armies. "And guard yourselves as to your spirit, and you must not deal treacherously.

When we look at these verses, we can better understand how we break the heart of God. Your wife is your companion and wife by covenant! When you marry you enter into an agreement with God beloved! God made you one with her! Not only that - He gave a portion of His Spirit in the union! He was seeking godly offspring! It is quite disturbing to see the casualness with which leaders of the faith throw away their covenant agreements with God. They fail to guard themselves in the spirit and the flesh creeps in. But the key here is verse 13. They cover the altar with tears and groaning because somehow the power of God has left them. If we do not understand the relationship in the spiritual realm between our covenants with God and the power that He can impart in our lives, then we are truly lost. God doesn't want to see our tears regarding not having our desires met when we are faithless in the things we have promised Him. I know many like to point to what Jesus said on the subject, but they misconstrue that as well:

Matthew 5:31-32 Updated American Standard Version (UASV)

³¹ "It was said, 'Whoever divorces his wife away, let him give her a certificate of divorce';[70] ³² but I say to you that everyone who divorces

---

[67] I.e. *offspring*
[68] Lit *he hates*
[69] Lit *sending away*
[70] A quotation from Deut. 24:1

his wife, except on the ground of sexual immorality,[71] makes her commit adultery; and whoever marries a divorced woman commits adultery.

What is Jesus teaching about here? Divorce? No - adultery. He is teaching that if you divorce for any other reason you become an adulterer in your following marriage and make an adulteress of your next wife! This is not a get out of jail free card beloved. God always hates divorce.[72] But preacher, you don't know my marriage. That is true. I am only saying what the Bible says. The real truth is that sometimes we do not take the covenant of marriage seriously enough *before* we get married. One of the greatest fears we have is being alone and we let that drive us into the arms of people God never intended for us to be with. There is a reason why the Bible implores us to not be unequally yoked:

2 Corinthians 6:14 Updated American Standard Version (UASV)

14 Do not be yoked together with unbelievers; for what partnership have righteousness and lawlessness, or what fellowship has light with darkness?

The answer to that question is NONE. There is no fellowship between light and darkness. That doesn't mean you cannot get along with someone. Years can go by seeming to prove the Word of God wrong and then...the testing comes. Every marriage goes through trials just like every person must. When those trials come, you will see there is no fellowship between light and darkness.

I am not saying these are easy teachings. I also present this as someone who has not been married. I try to take the act of entering into a covenant relationship with God very seriously. Reverently. One of the effects of the seeker-friendly theologies is a loss of reverence for the things of God in the church. There is no more teaching about the fear of the Lord. Easter bunnies on the altar of God. Secular leadership principles chased after by the church leaders. There is a cumulative effect. I have had people exclaim - "what's the big deal?" The big deal about the little lumps of leaven is eventually they spread throughout the entire batch. When we treat the little things of God as unimportant, or OK to compromise, eventually we start moving that bar. When we start compromising with the world we start to think like the world. We use their carnal logic instead of the Word of God. Maybe we look the other way about the faith of the person we want to marry,

---

[71] **Sexual Immorality:** (Heb. *zanah*; Gr. *porneia*) A general term for immoral sexual acts of any kind: such as adultery, prostitution, sexual relations between people not married to each other, homosexuality, and bestiality. – Num. 25:1; Deut. 22:21; Matt. 5:32; 1 Cor. 5:1.

[72] What is the Scriptural Basis for Divorce and Remarriage Among Christians? http://tiny.cc/arzzsy

after all, God doesn't want me alone! Maybe we look the other way when we are considering divorce - after all - God doesn't want me unhappy! This is how leaven works. Slowly and insidiously. The little things matter because they add up and pave the way towards the bigger things.

Lastly, on this subject, divorce is not an unpardonable sin beloved. Jesus died to cover our sins, and His grace is always sufficient. This is an instruction, not condemnation. Never walk under condemnation. Learn and move on. Learn and move on. God always has a new level for us to go to but it starts with treating the things of God with the reverence they are due. That has to start with those that would assume the leadership of the church. They are responsible for the spiritual development of the people. Their marriages should be an example for people to look to. That doesn't mean that their marriages are perfect but that the God who keeps them together is. What a radical thought in this postmodern world. That disagreements are not bigger than the God we serve. That the covenant is more important than our feelings. That the covenant still matters.

What does this have to do with tithing preacher? Everything. The reality is that many who preach tithing do so abusively and know they are lying. They know they are misrepresenting the Word of God. They have no fear of the Lord. They have no reverence. They make merchandise of the people of God. They do not honor the Levitical covenant or even their own marriage covenants sometimes. They do not view God as their Master but rather someone to use. It was important to lay this groundwork before getting to the third chapter. So, we understand where the Prophet Malachi was at when he penned that fateful chapter. The chapter so many abuse for filthy lucre.

So, we come to it. Malachi Chapter Three. More important to prosperity preachers than John 3:16 and dare I say it; more important to the vast majority of churches today as well. I guess it was bound to happen. We are carnal creatures who reflexively think with carnality. The further the modern church dives off the theological cliff the more carnal we become. The more we seek to be relevant to a culture that leads people to hell the more carnal we will think. The truth, however, is that this subject has roots deep down in church history. This has been the way the church has always operated. It is what the church has always taught. Over the centuries, the argument has been refined and polished to the point that even deep-thinking Christians often accept this slice of false teaching without so much as reading correct contextualized Scriptures or even daring to think about questioning it. It is the sacred cow of the church; the third rail if you will. It is tithing. The notion that God has instructed Christians to pay 10% of their income to the church as an act of obedience. The reality however when it comes to the topic of tithing is that leadership is only about 10% correct. They are in essence and quite possibly in ignorance, tithing the truth.

I love watching the snake oil salesmen on "Christian" television these days. They swear that no one is saying that you can buy a miracle from God. No one is saying that you can buy favor or blessing from God. Yet in the next sentence they are speaking all of this nonsense about sowing your seed, so you can reap a harvest! That is what you are saying! That is what the church is saying as well with their adherence to tithing. That is why it was embraced so universally. It is the essence of carnality when thinking about God. We believe that we can somehow control Him. That we can somehow buy Him off. I know pastors who have stripped lifelong church members of their membership because they didn't like their tithes. As if the church belonged to the pastor, and not Christ. I know other pastors who do not abuse the system. They preach once or twice a year about giving and never get involved with knowing who gave what. While that is far more palatable, the problem again is that there is no tithing requirement for the church, period.

I recognize this is touchy subject for many because we have been conditioned for so long to equate blessings to tithing. We have been wrongly taught that our tithe is the display of our obedience to God. I understand why that "sells" so well too. The truth is that tithing is the easiest form of obedience we actually have. Tithing allows us to maybe look the other way on the things we are not so obedient about. Like lust, pride, and hatred. We can always come back to the fact that they told us to give 10% and by gosh that's what we did. So we are obedient; kind of. Once again, the carnality of man's thinking. Man will gladly pay 10% of his income to think that the rest of his disobedience matters less. Or that the 10% garners him some kind of favor with God. A Spiritual quid pro quo. But I ask you for the next few pages to put aside your conventional thinking. Put aside the myths that you have been taught and consider. Read the Scriptures for yourselves.

Malachi 3:1-5 Updated American Standard Version (UASV)

3 "Look! I am sending my messenger, and he will prepare a way before me.[73] And suddenly the true Lord, whom you are seeking, will come to his temple; and the messenger of the covenant will come, in whom you take delight. Look, he will certainly come," says Jehovah of armies. 2 But

---

[73] John the Baptizer was the 'messenger who cleared up or prepared the way.' (Matt. 11:10-11)

who can endure the day of his coming, and who can stand when he appears? For he is like the fire of a refiner and like the soap of laundrymen.[74] 3 He will sit as a refiner and purifier of silver,[75] and he will purify the sons of Levi and refine them like gold and silver, and they will present offerings in righteousness to Jehovah. 4 Then the offering of Judah and Jerusalem will be pleasing to Jehovah as in the days of old and as in former years.

5 "Then I will draw near to you for judgment. I will be a swift witness against the sorcerers,[76] against the adulterers, against those who swear falsely, against those who oppress the hired worker in his wages, the widow and the fatherless, against those who thrust aside the foreigner,[77] and do not fear me, says Jehovah of armies.

Wait a minute preacher! This isn't the God they talk about at my church! Exactly. That is the point. For the first two chapters Malachi lays out his charges against the spiritual leaders of Israel but he is not done yet. Now comes the real prophecies. Not the candy-coated clairvoyance we get today. God is like a refiner's fire! He draws near for judgment. God is a God of justice. He cares for those that no one cares for. He cares for the oppressed worker. He cares for the widow and the fatherless. Those who are entrusted with the spiritual support of the people should never be found to be the ones who abuse them. And now we come to the key verses. We will examine them separately.

Malachi 3:6 Updated American Standard Version (UASV)

6 "For I, Jehovah, do not change; therefore you, O sons of Jacob, are not consumed.

After two and a half blistering chapters detailing how we do not honor our end of the covenants we have with God, He reminds us how far above us He is. After all of this, He does not change. He will always honor His end of the bargain. If He did change...if He treated us as we treated Him, we would be consumed. We would be destroyed. The refiner's fire may burn. It may hurt. But it does not seek to destroy but rather to purify. Our gospel today needs purification.

---

[74] One who in Bible times washed used clothing, removing impurities and unclean elements.
[75] Jehovah's fiery examination of "the sons of Levi" by the messenger of the covenant produces their cleansing.
[76] These ones were specialists in spells and incantations.
[77] Or *aliens, strangers, sojourners*

Malachi 3:7 Updated American Standard Version (UASV)

⁷ From the days of your fathers you have turned aside from my statutes and have not kept them. Return to me, and I will return to you, says Jehovah of armies. But you say, 'How shall we return?'

Our disobedience is nothing new. God's remedy is always simple. Return to Him and He will return unto us. What is important to note here however is the Pharisaical spirit that asks how shall we return? They are not asking out of curiosity or conviction but rather out of incredulity. The same way in the sixth verse of chapter one they asked, "How have we despised Your name?" The leaders simply do not believe the charges against them. Just like when Jesus preached against the Pharisees they never accepted anything He said about them. They were incredulous to the charges. The same holds true today for false teachers and even those who merely are caught up under the tithing deception. It is very difficult to break through with the truth. You can point out where their error is, but they mostly will refuse to see it. When confronted by his lack of using the Bible, Joel Osteen brushed the charge aside by saying he doesn't need to apologize for not bringing a Scripture in until the end of his messages. How shall we return? When criticized for his many heresies, Benny Hinn lamented that he wished he could find a Bible verse that allowed him to kill his critics. How have we despised Your name? Keep in mind this is still the leaders talking back to God. The dialogue motif established in chapter one has not changed.

Malachi 3:8 Updated American Standard Version (UASV)

⁸ Will a human dare to rob God? Yet you are robbing me! And you say, 'How have we robbed you?' In the tenth parts[78] and the offerings.

Will man rob God? Yet you are robbing me. But you say, 'How have we robbed you?' In your tithes and contributions. - Malachi 3: 8 (ESV)

Does this verse mean what today's tithing preachers say it means? Is this somehow relatable to the people not tithing correctly and thus robbing God? Without the benefit of the whole context of Malachi, it is easy to see how this can be twisted, but Malachi is still addressing the spiritual leaders, not the people. This is God answering the question from the previous verse asked by the priests. Scripture does not exist in a vacuum. Most leaders today start at verse eight and ignore the entire context leading up to it! For further proof, we turn to a cross-reference found in the 13th chapter of Nehemiah. Malachi was prophesying during the period of Nehemiah.

---

[78] I.e. *tithes*

FLEECING THE FLOCK

Nehemiah 13:4-14 Updated American Standard Version (UASV)

⁴ Now before this, Eliashib the priest, who was appointed over the chambers of the house of our God, and who was related to⁷⁹ Tobiah, ⁵ prepared for Tobiah a large chamber where they had previously put the grain offering, the frankincense, the vessels, and the tenth of grain, wine, and oil, which were given by commandment to the Levites, singers, and the gatekeepers, and the offerings of the priests. ⁶ During all of this, I was not in Jerusalem, for in the thirty-second year of Artaxerxes king of Babylon I went to the king. And after some time I asked leave of the king ⁷ and I came to Jerusalem, and I then discovered the evil that Eliashib had done for Tobiah, by preparing for him a chamber in the courts of the house of God. ⁸ It was very displeasing to me, and I threw all the household goods of Tobiah out of the chamber. ⁹ Then I gave orders, and they cleansed the chambers, and I brought back there the vessels of the house of God, with the grain offering and the frankincense.

¹⁰ I also found out that the portions of the Levites had not been given to them, so that the Levites and the singers, who did the work, had fled each to his field. ¹¹ So I confronted the officials and said, "Why is the house of God forsaken?" And I gathered them together and set them in their stations. ¹² Then all Judah brought the tenth of the grain, wine, and oil into the storehouses. ¹³ And I appointed as treasurers over the storehouses Shelemiah the priest, Zadok the scribe, and Pedaiah of the Levites, and as their assistant Hanan the son of Zaccur, son of Mattaniah, for they were considered reliable, and their duty was to distribute to their brothers. ¹⁴ Remember me, O my God, concerning this, and do not wipe out my good deeds that I have done for the house of my God and for his service.

Eliashib was the high priest but when Nehemiah was away he was robbing God. He was taking the tithes and offerings and not adhering to the system. He was cheating the Levites of their share and profaning the temple by allowing Tobiah in. Nehemiah straightened everything out when he got back but when you cross-reference this to the Prophet Malachi, it remains easy to see that the message is not towards the people but rather the spiritual leadership.

Malachi 3:9 Updated American Standard Version (UASV)

⁹ You are cursed with a curse, for you are robbing me, the whole nation of you.

---

⁷⁹ *close to*

This is the only place where it appears that the message is for everyone in Israel; the whole nation of you. There are three considerations however. The first is that the King James reads differently:

Malachi 3:9 King James Version (KJV)

⁹ Ye are cursed with a curse: for ye have robbed me, even this whole nation.

Even this whole nation does not indicate that they were robbing but rather that they were being robbed. This is supported by the Nehemiah verses where the people correctly brought their tithes and offerings only to have the leadership misappropriate them. Even if this translation is incorrect, there are two other considerations. One is that the nation is cursed because of the actions of the leadership. There is a reason why we are to be careful in whom we allow into leadership positions. The third consideration is that some commentaries seem to agree that this is merely a trickledown effect. That the people saw the leadership not care about tithes and offerings, so they followed suit. Here are comments from two different commentaries:

> **3:9** This accusation that **the whole nation** robs Yahweh in tithes and offerings fits the historical context of Malachi's ministry. Nehemiah 13:10 indicates that the people's failure to bring the tithes is an act that forces the Levites to leave their ministry and work in the fields to support themselves. Such neglect of the tithe is tantamount to robbery and has resulted in a curse. The rendering of the NIV (**You are under a curse**) does not translate the force of the Hebrew text, where the verb "curse" appears with its cognate noun. The NRSV approaches a more exact representation ("You are cursed with a curse"), but the Hebrew text is still more emphatic ("You are cursed with the curse"). "The curse" (see comments on Mal 2:2 above) is a likely allusion to the covenant curses of Deuteronomy 28:15–68 ("the curse" appears elsewhere only in Deut 28:20). Among these curses are agricultural disasters, which are the result of the disobedience of the postexilic community (Hag 1:4–6, 10–11; 2:16–17).[80]
>
> **3:9** This verse amplifies the charge that Judah was robbing God by pointing out two additional facts. The first is that they were doing this even though, like the Levites in 2:2, God had already begun to discipline

---

[80] Clay Ham and Mark Hahlen, *Minor Prophets*, The College Press NIV Commentary (Joplin, MO: College Press Pub. Co., 2001–), 566.

them with the curses he had warned them about a thousand years before (and as he had disciplined them time after time since then). "You are under a curse" uses a participle and could be more literally translated "by the curse you are being cursed." The verse begins in Hebrew with two clauses in strong and almost poetic contrast. Each clause contains three words, the second word being the pronoun "you" (plural), and the last word being a verb ending in the sound -*îm* (i.e., a masculine plural participle). The clauses can be literally rendered:

By-the-curse you are-being-cursed,

yet-me you are-robbing.

In spite of the self-destructive nature of their behavior, they continued inviting the divine curses of Deut 28:15–68 by plundering the divine storehouse. The painful experiences referred to here are perhaps first alluded to in 1:9, then again in 2:13 and in 2:17. Not until 3:11 is a specific difficulty mentioned—something was devouring their crops. Whether that was their only crisis we do not know. But clearly their failure to give what they owed to God was resulting in his withholding from them what they thought he owed them.

The second additional fact added by v. 9 to the accusation of v. 8 is that the entire nation was guilty. Outside the syntactical symmetry of the two clauses just examined is a noun phrase at the end of the verse that is in apposition to the "you" of those clauses—"the nation, all of it." Such awkward Hebrew has invited attempts to correct the text, but this grammatical device was well known to the book's author, who also used it in 1:7, 12. Its function is to call attention to the clause where it is found and to emphasize here that Judah's waywardness was not limited to a few. The whole nation was guilty before God and therefore was in a dangerous spot.[35] Were it not for the Lord's faithfulness, of which he reminded them even at the beginning of the prophecy, Israel would be ruined (see also 3:6).

Although Israel is typically referred to as a "people" rather than a "nation" and the term "nation" is sometimes used of Israel in a derogatory sense (Zeph 2:1), this is not always the case (Exod 19:6; Zeph 2:9). Therefore, although Malachi's use of the term could mean that Israel was acting toward the Lord the way all the nations acted, disregarding his ownership of all things, this understanding is tenuous.

3:10a As the paragraph begins in v. 7 with a reason (Israel's turning away) followed by a command (to return) with a result (God's return), so it ends in vv. 8–10 with a reason (Israel's robbing God) followed by a command with a result. The command is for God's people to "bring the whole tithe into the storehouse," and the result is "that there may be food in my house."

As Hill explains, the reference to the "storehouse" is to "an extended hallway divided into numerous rooms or cubicles ... for storage of tithes consisting of grain, wine, and (olive) oil." The phrase "the whole tithe" is almost identical to that which occurs in Lev 27:30, "*Every tenth* of the land's produce, grain from the soil or fruit from the trees, belongs to the Lord," and Num 18:21, "I have given the Levites *every tenth* in Israel as an inheritance" (HCSB). But an even closer parallel is found in Deut 14:28, "At the end of every three years, *bring all the tithes* [lit. "tithe"; but a different word for "bring" is used there] of that year's produce and store it in your towns" (similarly Deut 26:12). Specifying "the whole tithe" suggests that many were either withholding part of the tithe or were bringing nothing.[39] Reference to the "whole" tithe also echoes the guilt of the "whole" nation in v. 9.

Immediately following in Deut 14:29 is the purpose—"so that the Levites (who have no allotment or inheritance of their own) and the aliens, the fatherless and the widows who live in your towns may come and eat and be satisfied, and so that the Lord your God may bless you in all the work of your hands." This is clearly the background for the twin purposes of "food" (or "nourishment") in Mal 3:10a and divine blessing in vv. 10b–12. The interpretation of "food" as intended for the priests and Levites is made explicit in the Aramaic Targum, which renders "and there shall be *provision for those who serve in my Sanctuary*" (see also 2 Chr 31:4–10). The term "storehouse" (lit. "house of treasure") is also used in Neh 10:38[Hb. 39]: "A priest descended from Aaron is to accompany the Levites when they receive the tithes, and the Levites are to bring a tenth of the tithes up to the house of our God, to the storerooms of the *treasury*." A similar phrase is also used in Neh 12:44: "At that time men were appointed to be in charge of the storerooms for the contributions, firstfruits and tithes. From the fields around the towns they were to bring into the storerooms the portions required by the Law for the priests and the Levites, for Judah was pleased with the ministering priests and Levites."

Caring for landless inhabitants, especially the Levites, involved more than a lesson in compassion. As the Nazirites were to be occasional reminders that Israel was to be holy and dedicated to the Lord (Num 6:1–21), the Levites were to be a constant reminder that Israel was to be dependent on the Lord. Millar, stressing a point made previously by

> McConville, explains that "Israel's spiritual appropriation of the inheritance can come only when she sees the landless Levite, with only the Lord himself to enjoy, and models her life on him." Therefore, "the function of Levi in the land is to remind Israel that her ultimate calling is not merely to enjoy its produce, but relationship with him." So "if the Levites are neglected, it is not simply a sign of disobedience, but of a falling away from the relationship which the Levites themselves model."[81]

> *"the sin was become general, and therefore a general judgment was inflicted on them: Grotius thinks, that the people seeing the priests withhold the tithes from the Levites, they refused to pay them to them, and so the sin became universal. Kimchi observes, that in other sins charged upon the nation, the people were not all alike guilty, but in this which respected the tithes and offerings they were."*

The people saw how leadership was not complying - so they followed suit. We see this today in the modern church as well. Leaders preach holiness but then fall from grace and what lessons are learned in the congregation? Or they preach kindness and then treat people with disdain. But again - what were the people here guilty of? They were guilty of not tithing correctly, agricultural proceeds, during a period of time when tithing was the system for ensuring the Levites had food. One of the most fundamental rules of hermeneutics is that the Bible confirms itself. Where else in the Bible do we see anything remotely indicating that the few sentences found in the middle of a book written to the leading priests of Nehemiah's day should somehow be New Testament doctrine? Nowhere.

Verse nine also states that the people are now under a curse because of their lack of compliance. We know that Jesus broke all of the curses for those who have faith in Him. In order to believe that these portions of Malachi now are applicable to Christians today means we must apply the entire context. You cannot cherry pick Scriptures here and there and create doctrine where none exists. That is what cults do. We cannot be found in our position in Christ and His imputed righteousness and at the same time be cursed for not tithing correctly. Nor can we claim blessings as a result of our tithing. We are blessed because of our position in Christ not because of our adherence to one of the 613 Mosaic laws.

---

[81] Richard A. Taylor and E. Ray Clendenen, *Haggai, Malachi*, vol. 21A, The New American Commentary (Nashville: Broadman & Holman Publishers, 2004), 418–421.

Malachi 3:10 Updated American Standard Version (UASV)

[10] Bring all the tenth parts[82] into the storehouse, that there may be food in my house. And thereby put me to the test, says Jehovah of armies,[83] if I will not open the windows of heaven for you and pour down for you a blessing until there is nothing lacking.

Here is one of the most abused Scriptures in the entire Bible. Beloved, you simply cannot allegorize in order to create principles. Let me explain. There are principles of God that we need to adhere to. They are laid out in Scripture and are not ambiguous. We saw one already in this book when it comes to sowing and reaping. We saw that in Proverbs, a general principle is laid out about he who tends to scatter versus he who tends to withhold. Then we saw in 2Corinthians that principle established as the framework for New Testament giving. Lastly, we saw it reiterated when it comes to non-giving matters such as sowing to the flesh or the spirit. When it comes to Malachi 3:10 however, tithing preachers want to take a verse that has specific meanings and allegorize it to today. They want to pretend that the whole tithe means you must not give to anyone but your church. They want to pretend that the storehouse today means the church you attend. They want to pretend that God wants you to test Him in your tithing. They want to pretend that the windows of heaven mean untold blessings of indeterminate substance await the faithful tither. They want to pretend that God is just waiting to pour these fantastic blessings out into your life if you would just pay Him first. Of course, it is couched in pious talk about spiritual sounding matters such as "obedience," but the bottom line of the deal is always money. Let's go through each of these points of pretending.

The whole tithe deception is first. Tithing preachers use this phrase to convince congregants today that they must bring their ten percent only to

---

[82] I.e. *the full tithe*. The Mosaic Law was eliminated by Jesus' death, so monetary tithing is no longer a requirement. However, tithing has a figurative meaning. (Eph. 2:15) It does not symbolize the giving of our all. While the tenth part was brought every year, Christians now bring their all to the Father only once, when they dedicate themselves to him and symbolize their dedication by being water in water. It is whatever our situations allow, and our heart motivates us to use. The offerings we bring to the Father can be time, energy, and resources used in our carrying out the will of the Father, which would include attending Christian meetings, visiting sick ones and the elderly believers, and offering whatever financial support our heart moves us to give to God.

[83] **Jehovah of armies:** (Heb. *jhvh tsaba*) literally means an army of soldiers, or military forces (Gen. 21:22; Deut. 20:9). It can also be used figuratively, "the sun and the moon and the stars, all the armies of heaven." (Deut. 4:19) In the plural form, it is also used of the Israelites forces as well. (Ex. 6:26; 7:4; Num. 33:1; Psa. 44:9) However, the "armies" in the expression "Jehovah of armies" is a reference to the angelic forces primarily, if not exclusively.

the church that they attend. Then after that, they are allowed to "freely give" to other Christian causes. I have heard local pastors say that if you give your tithe to another ministry effort then do not bother asking him to perform a funeral or visit you in the hospital. How disgustingly sick. Does this notion actually line up with the remainder of Scripture? Does the Bible present a God that demands you first give ten percent of your money to a church building and then if there are leftovers to possibly help people in need?

Acts 2:42-47 Updated American Standard Version (UASV)

[42] And they continued devoting themselves to the teaching of the apostles and to fellowship, to the breaking of bread and to prayers.[84] [43] And fear came on every soul, and many wonders and signs were being performed through the apostles. [44] And all those who believed were together and had all things in common; [45] and they began selling their property and possessions and distributing these things to all, as anyone had need. [46] Day by day continuing with one mind in the temple, and breaking bread from house to house, they were taking their food together with gladness and sincerity of heart, [47] praising God and having favor with all the people. And the Lord added to their number day by day those who were being saved.

James 1:26-27 Updated American Standard Version (UASV)

[26] If any man thinks he is religious and does not bridle his tongue but deceives his heart, this person's religion is worthless. [27] Pure and undefiled religion before[85] our God and Father is this: to visit orphans and widows in their affliction, and to keep oneself unstained by the world.

These verses from the Book of Acts show us the model of the early church. The key in these verses is "as any had need." Now many in leadership today will tell you that this role is now under the province of the church, but anyone who has been in church long enough knows, obtaining money from the "Benevolence Ministry" can be quite arduous. Additionally, I have seen local churches literally strip memberships from people over tithing, even if they had solid record of giving in the past. This is the problem with misusing the "whole tithe" portion of this Scripture. It gives leadership the idea that the people are required to give them 10% and they hold no responsibility to them after that transaction. The James verse is possibly more telling of what lies in the heart of God. He clearly delineates for us the contrast between worthless religion and pure, undefiled religion. Worthless religion is centered upon a deceived heart. A

---

[84] Lit *the prayers*
[85] Or *in the sight of*

heart for example that can read a book such as Malachi and think it commands them to browbeat their sheep for money. Yet what is pure and undefiled religion? That which seeks to take care of the neediest in our society. There is no mention of money or tithing in these verses to explain what pure religion ought to be. If anything, it is the opposite. What did Jesus teach?

Matthew 25:31-46 Updated American Standard Version (UASV)

31 "When the Son of man comes in his glory, and all the angels with him, then he will sit down on his glorious throne. 32 All the nations will be gathered before him, and he will separate people one from another, just as a shepherd separates the sheep from the goats. 33 And he will put the sheep on his right hand, but the goats on his left.

34 "Then the King will say to those on his right: 'Come, you who have been blessed by my Father, inherit the Kingdom prepared for you from the founding of the world. 35 For I became hungry and you gave me something to eat; I was thirsty and you gave me something to drink. I was a stranger and you received me hospitably; 36 naked and you clothed me. I fell sick and you looked after me. I was in prison and you visited me.' 37 Then the righteous ones will answer him with the words: 'Lord, when did we see you hungry and feed you, or thirsty and give you something to drink? 38 When did we see you a stranger and receive you hospitably, or naked and clothe you? 39 When did we see you sick or in prison and visit you?' 40 In reply the King will say to them, 'Truly I say to you, to the extent that you did it to one of the least of these my brothers, you did it to me.'

41 "Then he will say to those on his left: 'Go away from me, you who have been cursed, into the eternal fire prepared for the Devil and his angels. 42 For I became hungry, but you gave me nothing to eat; and I was thirsty, but you gave me nothing to drink. 43 I was a stranger, but you did not receive me hospitably; naked, but you did not clothe me; sick and in prison, but you did not look after me.' 44 Then they too will answer with the words: 'Lord, when did we see you hungry or thirsty or a stranger or naked or sick or in prison and did not minister to you?' 45 Then he will answer them, saying: 'Truly I say to you, to the extent that you did not do it to one of these least ones, you did not do it to me.' 46 And these will go away into eternal punishment,[86] but the righteous into eternal life."

For all the preacher bluster about being cursed they need to read these verses. Cursed are those who do not help the needy. Who do not clothe the naked, feed the hungry and visit the prisoner. Jesus does not say come

---

[86] That is eternal cutting off, from life. Lit., "lopping off; pruning."

inherit the kingdom to those who tithed correctly. Those who brought the "whole tithe" to their local church. It simply flies in the face of Scripture as a whole. The next allegory they want to sell you is that the storehouse is your local church. To further this point, preachers will often refer to another New Testament verse containing the word "store."

1 Corinthians 16:1-4 Updated American Standard Version (UASV)

16 Now concerning the collection for the holy ones: as I directed the congregations of Galatia, so you also are to do. ² On the first day of the week, each of you is to put something aside and store it up, as he may prosper,[87] so that there will be no collecting when I come. ³ And when I arrive, whomever you may approve, I will send them with letters to carry your gift to Jerusalem; ⁴ And if it seems advisable that I should go also, they will travel with me.

Putting aside the silliness of playing word games, this proves nothing regarding tithing and everything regarding sacrificial New Testament model giving. Remember, we should give into the work of the kingdom. We should give to help those in need. James teaches us what good does it do to see someone in need and offer him pious platitudes? Faith without works is dead. That aside, what is really going on in these 1Corinthian verses? Paul is taking up a collection for the poor believers in Jerusalem. He does not want to be delayed when he comes, so he gives instruction for the collection. Nowhere does it mention tithe. Nowhere does it mention ten percent. This is, in fact, the model for New Testament giving found in 2Corinthians 9. To give cheerfully and to help those in need. Either way, there is zero evidence that God wrote Malachi 3 and intended for anyone to allegorize a literal storehouse where food went, into the New Testament church.

The next stop on this allegory is "test me." We all know how this is preached. The pastor will swear this is the only place in the Bible where God challenges you to test Him. They must forget Romans 12:2 and our command to test and approve what His will is. This "test me" theology, however, is then multiplied as the preacher twists it to try and mean that God wants you to test Him with your tithe. This is wrong on many levels. First of all, it sets up a quid-pro-quo notion. I have seen heretics such as Robert Morris now offering "tithing challenges" to their congregants. Tithe for a specific period and if you are not satisfied with what God does for you, he promises to give you your money back. This is just plain evil in design. First of all, anything positive at all that happens will immediately be credited to the tithe. Your kid got an A? Yeah, that's because you tithed.

---

[87] I.e. according to his own means

You received your tax return early? Yeah, that's because you tithed. Anything vaguely positive happened? Of course! It is all because you tithed. What about those who go through this period and see no "blessings." They, in fact, go through trials of some sort. Realize that the scam does not need everyone to be suckered. It is like the scam run by people in the sports betting business. They call up 100 people claiming to have inside information on the game tonight, and they are giving it to you for free. They give 50 one side and 50 the other. The 50 who lose, who cares? The 50 who wins though, now they think you have inside information, and now you can charge for it. In the church scam, all 100 were not tithing, to begin with. So even if only 50 believe they were "blessed" because of the tithing challenge; that is still 50 more tithers than you previously had.

What is God really telling His people here in verse 10? This is a reference back to the Mosaic Law, of which, tithing was only one. Go back and read Deuteronomy 28 and you will see the many blessings God promises for obedience to the law, including:

Deuteronomy 28:12 Updated American Standard Version (UASV)

^{12} Jehovah will open for you his good storehouse, the heavens, to give rain to your land in its season and to bless all the work of your hand; and you shall lend to many nations, but you shall not borrow.

This is the same "throw open the windows of heaven" promise we see here in verse ten. In a land where drought was plentiful, God is very clearly promising abundance of crops through rain, which He will pour out if His people would just be obedient. Test Him? The entire law was God saying, test me! It was a test the Israelites failed over and over again. Not only that but read the last 58 verses of Deuteronomy 28, and you will see nothing but the curses for disobedience. You cannot pluck tithing out from the Mosaic Law and stand it alone. The law did not work like that. You had to keep all of it, or you were guilty of breaking all of it. That was why no one could do it. That is why God had to send Jesus Christ to earth, to begin with! But to hear preachers misuse this verse, God carried over tithing as a law requirement while discarding the remaining 612 Mosaic Laws and that is ridiculous. Not only that but what about Jesus Christ?

Acts 15:10-11 Updated American Standard Version (UASV)

^{10} Now therefore why do you put God to the test by placing upon the neck of the disciples a yoke which neither our fathers nor we have been able to bear? ^{11} But we believe that we will be saved through the grace of the Lord Jesus, in the same way they are."

FLEECING THE FLOCK

Tithing preachers need to read this as if it is written directly to them. Why are you putting God to the test by placing yokes around the necks of your sheep? Yokes that our fathers could not bear. Yokes that Christ nailed to the cross on our behalf? Just believe that we will be saved through Him. Not to mention the elephant in the tithing room. Did Jesus save us from the law or not? In order for the tithing system to be carried over for believers today, we would have to believe that God sent Christ to die to blot out our sins for breaking 612 laws but not tithing? Plus He would have to change His system of breaking one law breaks them all? From a God, we know never changes?

Next, we have to believe that when God says He will throw open the heavens, He is making a promise of blessing in return for your tithe. Now, every tithing pastor is sharp enough to say that "you can't buy blessings" but that is exactly what they are selling! The allegory is ridiculous! God is up in heaven with the windows closed, but if you would just give your church 10% of your income, He will open those windows just for you! You can't buy blessing, but we sure can sell them! Only they are either mistaken or lying. This verse deals with a Prophet talking to the disobedient priests in the days of Nehemiah. It is not meant to be allegorized and carried into the New Testament. It is still part of the civil law, which was only for the management of a now defunct theocracy. No beloved, God is not shutting the windows of heaven against you for not tithing.

Philippians 4:14-20 Updated American Standard Version (UASV)

[14] Nevertheless, you have done well to share [88] with me in my affliction.

[15] And you yourselves also know Philippians that in the beginning of the gospel, when I left Macedonia, no congregation[89] shared with me in the matter of giving and receiving but you alone. [16] For even in Thessalonica you sent gifts for my needs once and again.[90] [17] Not that I seek the gift, but I seek the fruit that increases to your account. [18] But I have received everything in full, and I have an abundance. I am fully supplied, having received from Epaphroditus what you sent a fragrant aroma, an acceptable sacrifice, well-pleasing to God. [19] And my God will supply every need of yours according to his riches in glory in Christ Jesus. [20] Now to our God and Father be the glory forever and ever.[91] Amen.

---

[88] Or *have fellowship with*
[89] Gr *ekklesia* ("assembly")
[90] Lit "and once and twice"
[91] Lit *to the ages of the ages*

I have seen tithing pastors use this set of verses as well even though it proves the opposite of tithing! Paul does not say it was required of them to share in his trouble. We also see that no other church entered into a giving partnership with him! Were they all being disobedient to the tithing requirement? If so, why didn't Paul rebuke them for it? Then he says he was not even seeking the gift! That doesn't sound like the compulsory tithing system that is preached today at all. Then the verse we all know. Our God will supply all of our needs according to how well we tithe? No. According to His riches in glory in Christ Jesus. God cannot be bought beloved. He is not for sale. Malachi proves this when it is read in the correct context and you do not make silly allegories. Let us return to the Malachi text.

Malachi 3:11-12 Updated American Standard Version (UASV)

¹¹ I will rebuke the devourer for you, so that it will not destroy the fruits of your soil, and your vine in the field will not fail to bear, says Jehovah of armies. ¹² Then all nations will call you blessed, for you will be a land of delight, says Jehovah of armies.

Pat Robertson was asked a question on his show this year by an elderly woman whose husband was in the hospital, if it would be OK to pay the hospital bill with her tithe. His answer was that the reason why her husband was in the hospital was because he was being attacked by the devourer and you know the only way to have God rebuke the devourer is to tithe. So his actual guidance was to pay her tithe and not the hospital bill for her sick husband. Besides the repulsive nature of this advice, it should not be surprising. This is the nonsense you hear from the pulpits every week across this country. Overflowing blessings if you give me your money or else the devourer is coming for you! Do you know what the devourer actually is? Here is the explanation from Old Testament Commentary:

Joel 1:4 Updated American Standard Version (UASV)

⁴ What the cutting locust left, the swarming locust has eaten. What the swarming locust left, the hopping locust has eaten, and what the hopping locust left, the destroying locust has eaten.

> 1:4. How do you describe what is happening? You have to come up with every kind of locust you ever heard of and describe what each has done. This is not just one small group of locusts; this is the congregation of all the locusts that have ever invaded the land. The pattern of one type of locust eating what previous locusts had left is reminiscent of the language of Exodus 10:5,15 where locusts ate what the hail had left in the Egyptian plagues.

> Identifying the different types of locusts is, as Stuart notes, "speculative" (p. 241). Garrett concludes: "Beyond the fact that they all in some way refer to locusts, we simply do not know what these four words denote" (NAC, 316). The locust swarm may refer to an adult ready to fly on its own or to a caterpillar or to the smallest type of locust or the early grub stage of the locust. It appears in Joel 2:25 and in Amos 4:9.
>
> The great locusts apparently refers to migratory locusts with fully developed wings. Levitical laws permitted them as food (Lev. 11:22). Young locusts seems to be a creeping locust that is wingless (Jer. 51:14,27). Other locusts represents either some stage in the life of the locust or perhaps even a cockroach (Isa. 33:4).
>
> Whatever the exact designations of these crop destroyers, the point is intensified by using so many different names. All-consuming bugs filled the fields of Judah. Nothing escaped the voracious appetites of these invaders.
>
> Such locust invasions were not uncommon in Palestine, and they normally disappeared in a short time, so the prophet had to do something creative to magnify the image and make the people cringe at the thought of what was happening. This was not your usual locust invasion. This was eerie, mysterious—yes, supernatural. This was God caused. It could only be God ended. That is the major reason it needed to be stored up in national lore and added to the list of things God had done for his people.[92]

We tend to forget but tithing is an agricultural system, not a monetary system. As such, there are hordes of destroying, devouring menaces to crops. All of the other commentaries agree. The devourer is referring to insects that eat crops. God did not use this term, so it can be allegorized into any perceived threat in the life of a believer. Your company is downsizing? That must be the devourer! Your wife ran off with another man? That darn devourer is at it again! Your kid got his face pierced? If you would just tithe faithfully God would rebuke that ole devourer you got eating away at your life! I do not think we realize how silly things we believe are until we actually stop and do the work of a Berean. Jesus said that we would face tribulation in this life. Every negative thing is not "the devourer." Realize what they are saying here. Take the woman with the husband in the hospital for example. Are you honestly suggesting that God

---

[92] Butler, Trent. Holman Old Testament Commentary - Hosea, Joel, Amos, Obadiah, Jonah, Micah (Kindle Locations 3002-3019). B&H Publishing Group. Kindle Edition.

either made him sick or allowed him to become sick, because of tithing? Are you honestly suggesting that God wants to heal the man? He is dying to throw open those window, pour out healing blessings, and rebuke the cankerworm that is eating away at his health, but they haven't paid enough? How repugnant. Not to mention, here is the kicker. The woman asked if she could switch her tithe to pay the bill. That means she was tithing already. How did that nasty ole devourer end up striking her husband ill if she was correctly tithing already? It is all an elaborate, insidious allegorical scheme. God wants to bless you, but you have to pay first. You don't want the blessings? Well then, He will send the devourer after you for not paying them but one way or another, you're paying. But it is all worth it according to the tithing preacher. After all, you will be called blessed and be a land of delight! Not a bad bargain for only ten percent of your income!

Malachi 3:13-15 Updated American Standard Version (UASV)

[13] "Your words have been strong[93] against me, says Jehovah. But you say, 'How have we spoken against you?' [14] You have said, 'It is vain to serve God. What is the profit of our keeping his charge or of walking as in mourning before Jehovah of armies? [15] So now we call the arrogant blessed; not only are the doers of wickedness built up but they also test God and they escape.'"

If you listen to tithing preachers, Malachi ends at 3:12. The gambit has already been played by then. No need to muddy the money pitch by adding context. Yet 3:13-15 clearly shows that the narrative has not changed. God is still talking to the leaders and they are still answering Him like they have done nothing wrong. How have we spoken against you? By saying it is useless to serve God. By thinking you can get away with it. God calls them out here for what they have become; proud in their blatant disobedience. Ironically enough, these verses apply today to the very Christian leaders who misuse this great prophetic book to demand money from the sheep. Unlike the leaders however, no allegory is needed. For the tithing teachers are proud and arrogant in their defense of the indefensible. They put God to the test and think they escape. Safety in numbers they think. Everyone teaches tithing. They know all the right Scriptures but do not care to handle the Word correctly. They may have fooled themselves but God is never mocked. Remember, when you hear Malachi preached for tithing you only hear this:

---

[93] I.e. *hard* or *harsh*

Malachi 3:8-12 Updated American Standard Version (UASV)

⁸ Will a human dare to rob God? Yet you are robbing me! And you say, 'How have we robbed you?' In the tenth parts⁹⁴ and the offerings ⁹ You are cursed with a curse, for you are robbing me, the whole nation of you. ¹⁰ Bring all the tenth parts⁹⁵ into the storehouse, that there may be food in my house. And thereby put me to the test, says Jehovah of armies,⁹⁶ if I will not open the windows of heaven for you and pour down for you a blessing until there is nothing lacking. ¹¹ I will rebuke the devourer for you, so that it will not destroy the fruits of your soil, and your vine in the field will not fail to bear, says Jehovah of armies. ¹² Then all nations will call you blessed, for you will be a land of delight, says Jehovah of armies.

Even taken allegorically these verses can be pretty convincing to persuade someone that they need to hand over 10% of their income. The problem is it is only five verses out of 55 in the whole book. That is massive context missing. Now I am not suggesting that you must read every verse of a book just to have God speak about a particular set of verses. This however is different. This is used across Christendom as a principle God has laid out for us and it is simply untrue. Chapter Three concludes

Malachi 3:16-18 Updated American Standard Version (UASV)

¹⁶ Then those who feared Jehovah spoke to one another, and Jehovah gave attention and heard, and a book of remembrance⁹⁷ was written before him for those who fear Jehovah and for those thinking on⁹⁸ his name. ¹⁷ "And they will be mine," says Jehovah of armies, "on the day

---

⁹⁴ I.e. *tithes*

⁹⁵ I.e. *the full tithe*. The Mosaic Law was eliminated by Jesus' death, so monetary tithing is no longer a requirement. However, tithing has a figurative meaning. (Eph. 2:15) It does not symbolize the giving of our all. While the tenth part was brought every year, Christians now bring their all to the Father only once, when they dedicate themselves to him and symbolize their dedication by being water in water. It is whatever our situations allow, and our heart motivates us to use. The offerings we bring to the Father can be time, energy, and resources used in our carrying out the will of the Father, which would include attending Christian meetings, visiting sick ones and the elderly believers, and offering whatever financial support our heart moves us to give to God.

⁹⁶ **Jehovah of armies:** (Heb. *jhvh tsaba*) literally means an army of soldiers, or military forces (Gen. 21:22; Deut. 20:9). It can also be used figuratively, "the sun and the moon and the stars, all the armies of heaven." (Deut. 4:19) In the plural form, it is also used of the Israelites forces as well. (Ex. 6:26; 7:4; Num. 33:1; Psa. 44:9) However, the "armies" in the expression "Jehovah of armies" is a reference to the angelic forces primarily, if not exclusively.

⁹⁷ That book of remembrance is a record of all those who have served the Father in integrity. The Hebrew word for "remembrance" (*zik·kā·rôn*) involves more than just the action of calling something to mind. It can also indicate doing something about what is remembered. The Father will never forget his faithful servants.

⁹⁸ I.e. *meditating on*

when I prepare a treasured possession, and I will spare them as a man spares his son who serves him. ¹⁸ Then once more you will distinguish between the righteous and the wicked, between one who serves God and one who does not serve him.

Chapter Three closes with a contrast. There still were some who feared the Lord. This is an important point for us in this discussion. When we look out across the Christian landscape and see how many embrace this false teaching it can become disconcerting. Many who are deceivers and others who are simply deceived. The Bible teaches us this will only go from bad to worse:

2 Timothy 3:12-13 Updated American Standard Version (UASV)

¹² Indeed, all who desire to live godly in Christ Jesus will be persecuted. ¹³ But evil men and impostors will progress from bad to worse, deceiving and being deceived.

What is behind this is a loss of fear of the Lord. How else can you explain such shoddy hermeneutics from those who claim to have a divine call on their life? This is also the end result of purpose driven Warren Theology. When church becomes a business, and the pastor becomes a CEO, it is only a matter of time before money becomes the primary focus over our Lord and Savior Jesus Christ. To support visions God never gave. If you asked honest pastors who still teach tithing, they would probably say they are scared. Afraid that if they left it up to cheerful givers and the indwelt Holy Spirit that they would not pull in enough to keep their church doors open. It is sad really because that is no excuse to mangle the Word of God. Then there are those who know full well what they are doing. They need to read the fourth and final chapter of Malachi, where he prophesies the return of Christ and the Great Day of the Lord. Without this fear, these charlatans continue to abuse the sheep of God. The Bride of Christ. All for filthy lucre.

The truth is that as the church has seen more and more leaven infiltrating its walls we have seen carnal thinking explode exponentially. Chasing secular leadership principles. Employing non-biblical growth theories. But underlying all of them is the centuries old backdrop of tithing. It is founded and defended by a patchwork of Scriptures taken out of context and cobbled together by well-trained speakers to sell compulsory giving. Malachi, Chapter Three is at the top of that list. Listen, not everyone involved is even aware. I have seen otherwise solid biblical preachers jump off the theological cliff for the tithing deception. I know people who otherwise are completely sold out for Christ, yet this malformed tithing deception has been so deeply ingrained for them that just this writing alone will be anathema to them. As long as those who should know better refuse to see the Scriptural light, the truth will continue to be tithed.

CHAPTER SIX The Abram & Jacob Tithed Lies

While Malachi contains the primary Scriptures used to defend tithing, some pastors realized that people were starting to understand that it reinforces a system of the Mosaic Law that is no longer in effect and never applied to believers anyway. So, the search began to try and find other Scriptures to prop up this notion of New Testament tithing. We must understand this is centuries of false beliefs and teaching that has constructed a model for church maintenance. The fear amongst even the very best pastors is that changing this system mid-stream will result in such a drop off of giving that they would have to close their doors. Compounding this problem is the implementation of the purpose driven church model which the majority of churches follow today. Under this business plan, the church is a corporation, and the CEO is the pastor. He becomes responsible for the horizontal growth of the church, meaning the increase in the number of attendees. The reality, however, is God designed the church where He was responsible for that growth, so the pastor could remain committed to preaching the unvarnished Gospel resulting in the vertical growth of the sheep through discipleship:

Acts 2:42-47 Updated American Standard Version (UASV)

[42] And they continued devoting themselves to the teaching of the apostles and to fellowship, to the breaking of bread and to prayers.[99] [43] And fear came on every soul, and many wonders and signs were being performed through the apostles. [44] And all those who believed were together and had all things in common; [45] and they began selling their property and possessions and distributing these things to all, as anyone had need. [46] Day by day continuing with one mind in the temple, and breaking bread from house to house, they were taking their food together with gladness and sincerity of heart, [47] praising God and having favor with all the people. And the Lord added to their number day by day those who were being saved.

This is the model God lays out for us regarding the New Testament Church. What it has become in these last days is the opposite. I heard a mega church pastor recently preach that Jesus intended for the church to

---

[99] Lit *the prayers*

not feed the sheep but rather try and feed the unsaved. That is an absurd heresy. God does not want the sheep to starve. Jesus instructed Peter three times to feed His sheep. Well, what about the unsaved preacher? What about them? There is nothing the pastor is going to say to save them. Only the Gospel can do that. Only Jesus Christ has the words of eternal life. The unsaved sitting in a Gospel-centric church will either respond to the drawing of the Holy Spirit or they will not. Watering the Gospel down and dipping it in confectionary sugar will not save them. The Sinner's Prayer, which was already poor theology, has now become a punchline in a bad joke that condemns millions to hell. Here is the only time salvation is addressed in the Purpose Driven Life:

> *Wherever you are reading this, I invite you to bow your head and quietly whisper the prayer that will change your eternity: "Jesus I believe in you and receive you." Go ahead. If you sincerely meant that prayer, congratulations! Welcome to the family of God!* (Warren, 2002, pp. 58-59)

Jesus, I believe in you and receive you? Seriously? The devil believes in Jesus. Then to arrogantly welcome the person to the family of God? No repentance? No discussion of sin? Then they go find their purpose by serving in a ministry in their local church that continues to foster the notion they are saved when they are not. They stand before Christ at the end saying, "Lord Lord." If it were not so cruel it might be funny.

So, these factors combine in the purpose driven CEO-pastor to create a perfect tithing storm. He must enforce giving to keep fueling this model which is not from God. The bad ones wield it like a baton crushing the sheep under their dogma, while the better ones are less abusive but still enforce it. With Malachi often not being enough, we start to turn to the newer tithing lies starting with Abram and Jacob. You hear this quite often now from charlatan preachers. Abram and Jacob tithed before the law! Before we get to this it is important to understand the sleight of hand they are using. The tithing that preachers try to enforce is the Levitical system of tithing. This is the system that demanded 10% in a set pattern and system. They know full well that Abram and Jacob, who lived centuries before the Mosaic Law, never tithed in this manner; so, they try to pull a fast one. They lift up the one time the word tithe appeared in the lives of Abram and Jacob and based on that one-time event try to enforce the Levitical system of tithing. They have to do this because as we will see, neither Abram nor Jacob provide a model for tithing today. All the liars have done is strip mine the Bible for the word "tithe" and try to use that to create doctrine. Let us start with Abram:

Genesis 14:17-24 Updated American Standard Version (UASV)

¹⁷ After Abram returned from defeating Chedorlaomer and the kings who were with him, the king of Sodom went out to meet Abram at the Valley of Shaveh, that is, the Valley of the King. ¹⁸ And Melchizedek king of Salem brought out bread and wine; he was priest of the Most High[100] God. ¹⁹ He blessed him and said,

"Blessed be Abram by the Most High God,
Creator of heaven and earth;
²⁰ and blessed be the Most High God,
who has delivered your enemies[101] into your hand."

And he gave him a tenth of everything. ²¹ And the king of Sodom said to Abram, "Give me the souls, but take the goods for yourself." ²² But Abram said to the king of Sodom, "I have lifted up my hand[102] to Jehovah the Most High God, Creator of heaven and earth, ²³ that I will not take a thread or a sandal strap or anything that is yours, so that you may not say, 'I made Abram rich.' ²⁴ I will take nothing but what the young men have eaten, and the share of the men who went with me; Aner, Eshcol, and Mamre; let them take their share."

If pastors tried to present this as a model for giving, they would be sorely disappointed. Look at what has happened here. Abram is victorious in battle and a local pagan king, Melchizedek, comes to meet him after the battle. Abram gives him a tenth of the spoils of war. The word in Hebrew for tenth is generally rendered tithe. So technically, Abram gave a tithe to this king. If we keep reading, however, he actually ends up giving him all of the spoils, minus some food for his men. What are the implications for us when you compare this tithe to what the tithing preacher then tries to demand based upon this story? First of all, Abram did not tithe out of his personal wealth at all, which was substantial.

Genesis 13:2 Updated American Standard Version (UASV)

² Now Abram was very rich in livestock, in silver, and in gold.

Therefore, to use the Abram tithed model we would only tithe spoils of war and never out of our own wealth. Secondly however, Abram only tithed this one time in his entire life. Most commentators agree this tithe

---

[100] Heb ('ĕl·yôn) *El Elyon*
[101] **Adversaries:** (Heb. *tsarim*) An enemy, foe, adversary, or opponent, i.e., a personal enemy, who is in a state of open hostility or conflict. – Gen. 14:20; Num. 10:9; Ezra 4:1; Ps 44:5, 7.
[102] I.e., *I have taken an oath*

was probably customary to the local king. This tithe literally had nothing to do with God. When Abram gave the other 90%; that was all about God. He did not want a pagan king to be able to say that he made Abram rich. He wanted God alone to get the glory. He would not take a thread or sandal strap from this king. Some scurrilous preachers go as far as to say this is simply reinforcing a biblical principle. That is utter hogwash. God promised to make Abram's descendents as numerous as the stars without any demand for compensation. His instructions for faith were to leave his land and eventually sacrifice his son. No mention of tithing anywhere in these stories. God would not establish a universal principle this vague and unsubstantiated that would then be undone by the model for New Testament giving in 2Corinthians 9. We see this thread running through the depraved mind of abusive tithing preachers. That these random events, which had absolutely nothing to do with the Levitical tithing system, all establish a principle that you are to give them 10% of your income. When you do the work of a Berean though, their argument falls flat on its face. So, did Abram tithe? No. Not when the word is phrased like that. That is the sleight of hand. To say someone "tithed" implies we are talking about the Levitical system. Abram gave ten percent onetime to a local pagan king. If you want to use the Hebrew word tithe for that, fine but it establishes nothing. This ten percent was taken from the spoils of war. Never did Abram give any tithe from his personal wealth, which was considerable. This was a solitary event in an otherwise titheless life. It was not ordered by God, ordained by God, or remotely of God. It was probably a local custom. Additionally, Abram actually gave 100% of the spoils so that the king could not take credit for his prosperity and God alone could get the glory. Do not fall for the Abram tithed lie. So, what about Jacob?

Well, apparently tithing skips a generation in the minds of tithing fanatics because Isaac certainly never tithed. Skipping straight to Jacob however, we see the tithing pushers have even less of an argument than they had with Abram. Remember, these are held up as examples of why modern-day followers of Jesus Christ should participate in the Levitical tithing system. In this story we see the word tenth used again, which translates into Hebrew as tithe. This is seized upon by tithing preachers with complete disregard for context and haphazardly applied forward to the Levitical tithing system. So, what do we see in Jacob that led to this point in his life? Jacob was a deceiver from birth. He tricked his brother Esau out of his birthright of being the first born. This may not sound like a big deal today but in those days, it was a very big deal. The first born got untold blessings that the other children did not. Jacob also tricked his old and blind father into bestowing the blessing reserved for the first born, again at the expense of his brother. Before fleeing for his life, he received a further blessing from his father Isaac upon his seed, essentially passing down the promised blessing of Abraham onto his descendants. Despite these things, Jacob still has no confidence in himself or his relationship with God. He knows how he obtained everything. He knows he is a deceiver. Fleeing to Haran to escape the wrath of his brother, he has a dream:

Genesis 28:10-15 Updated American Standard Version (UASV)

[10] Then Jacob went out from Beersheba and went to Haran. [11] And he arrived at a certain place and spent the night there, because the sun had set. And he took one of the stones of the place and put it under his head and slept at that place. [12] And he dreamed, and look, there was a ladder set up on the earth, and the top of it reached to heavens; and look, the angels of God were ascending and descending on it. [13] And behold, Jehovah stood above it and said, "I am Jehovah, the God of Abraham your father and the God of Isaac; the land on which you lie I will give to you and to your seed.[103] [14] Your seed will be like the dust of the earth, and you will spread abroad to the west and to the east and to the north and to the south, and in you and your seed will all the families of the earth be blessed. [15] Look, I am with you and will keep you wherever you go, and will bring you back to this land; for I will not leave you until I have done what I have promised you."

What do we see here beloved? This is God essentially assuring Jacob that he is now the possessor of the promise made to his grandfather Abraham. This is God assuring Jacob. Yet what is missing? There is no mention of tithing, money, or anything Jacob would have to do for these blessings. There is no quid-pro-quo. There are no stipulations to the promises God is making. Does Jacob wake up with a renewed sense of faith? The kind of faith that Abraham was known for? Does he wake up confident now that God will be with him and see him through no matter what? Not even close.

Genesis 28:16-22 Updated American Standard Version (UASV)

[16] Then Jacob awoke from his sleep and said, "Surely Jehovah is in this place, and I did not know it." [17] And he was afraid and said, "How awesome is this place! This is none other than the house of God, and this is the gate of heaven."

[18] And Jacob rose early in the morning, and he took the stone that he had put under his head and set it up as a pillar, and poured oil on top of it. [19] He called the name of that place Bethel,[104] but the name of the city

---

[103] I.e. *offspring* or *descendants*
[104] I.e. the house of God

was Luz at the first. ²⁰ Then Jacob made a vow, saying, "If God will be with me and will keep me in this way that I go, and will give me bread to eat and garments to wear, ²¹ so that I come again to the house of my father in peace, then Jehovah will be my God, ²² This stone, which I have set up as a pillar, will be the house of God, and of all that you give me I will surely give a tenth to you."

There is that word tenth again! Once again, in the Hebrew it is translated as tithe. So tithing preachers latch onto it like they did in the story of Abram, but they are just as wrong. What do we see here in the text? Is this a model for New Testament giving? First of all, this text does not even say that Jacob tithed. It says that he promised he would. Nowhere in Scripture do we ever find out if he actually followed through on this promise. The Scriptural truth is we do not know if Jacob ever gave a tithe. More importantly however look at the essentials of this promise. Showing an utter lack of faith, completely unlike his father and grandfather, Jacob apparently does not believe God! He tries to play let's make a deal! He says if you really do what you promised me you would do, then I will make you my God and only then will I give you ten percent of all you give me. This is a completely conditional tithe! What kind of model is that? To truly preach this as a model for tithing, you would have to allow your congregants to make deals with God based solely upon a certain level of blessing that God must deliver first in order for the tithe to be released. There isn't a tithing preacher alive who would leave that up to the congregation so instead, they say Jacob tithed and try to then enforce the Levitical tithing system. It is complete rubbish. So, did Jacob tithe? No. He promised one time to give ten percent if God did certain things for him. This not a model for tithing and like we saw in the case of Abram, it does not set up a universal principle. God did not ask for nor demand a tithe from Jacob. God's promises were based on His covenant with Abraham. Jacob's promise of paying a tenth does not show obedience at all but rather doubt and unbelief. Furthermore, there is no Biblical proof that he ever actually followed through on this promise. To hold this up as anything regarding faithful giving for New Testament believers is fanciful at best and criminal at worst.

CHAPTER SEVEN The Jesus Taught Tithing Lie

As the tithing preachers become more desperate to hold onto a slice of your money, they become more obvious in their deception. I can understand how some are deceived by Malachi. If all you ever hear are those four verses instead of the surrounding four chapters of context it can be fairly convincing. Abram and Jacob might be tricky too because the word "tithe" does appear in both stories. Then we come to a lie that is far easier to debunk. The lie that Jesus taught tithing. This of course is untrue and in fact, there is no Scriptural evidence that Jesus Himself ever tithed. This may come as a shock to many but even under the Levitical system, not everyone was required to tithe. We know the poor were exempt but also so were nonagricultural producers. Craftsmen, for example, would instead appear at feast time with a freewill offering based upon their own individual financial circumstances:

Deuteronomy 16:16-17 Updated American Standard Version (UASV)

[16] "Three times a year all your males shall appear before Jehovah your God at the place that he will choose, at the Feast of Unleavened Bread, at the Feast of Weeks, and at the Feast of Booths, and hey shall not appear before the Lord empty-handed. [17] Every man shall give as he is able, according to the blessing of Jehovah your God that he has given you.

That sounds awful close to 2Corinthians 9! Principle of sowing and reaping. Nothing forced or compulsory. Jesus of course was a carpenter by trade and as such, would not be required to tithe. Yet what about the claim that He taught tithing. Let us as always turn to Scripture:

Matthew 23:23-24 Updated American Standard Version (UASV)

[23] "Woe to you, scribes and Pharisees, hypocrites! because you give the tenth of the mint and the dill and the cumin, but you have disregarded the weightier matters of the Law, namely, justice and mercy and faithfulness. These things it was necessary to do, yet not to disregard the other things. [24] Blind guides, who strain out a gnat and swallow a camel!

If you read these verses and the context of everything Jesus criticized the Pharisees for and come away with the lesson that we must tithe I would say you missed the points; all of them. This has nothing to do with tithing. Jesus is not teaching tithing, nor is He even reinforcing it. He is speaking to what they neglect and showing how their strict adherence to the Levitical tithing system had become a source of pride and a stumbling block to other sin in their lives. He accused them of becoming whitewashed tombs. Clean and pretty on the outside but full of filth and dead men's bones. The correlation to the abusive tithing system of today cannot be clearer. Many believers tithe but look past the weightier matters of obedience. Their secret sins get a pass because tithing justifies them in their wicked hearts. Maybe I flirt with the girl in the office but at least I am tithing! I have seen firsthand the prideful nature of many tithers today. They cannot see the falseness of the tithing message because they have bought into it and anyone who speaks against it is viewed as not paying their fair share. When you examine the surrounding woes, Jesus speaks to the Pharisees here it is clear that He used the illustration of tithing to highlight their hypocrisy, not to "teach tithing."

That said however, let us examine two other points that seemingly escape tithing teachers regarding these verses. First of all, what is it that Jesus mentions they tithe? Is it money? Is Jesus teaching that they need to tithe their shekels? Of course, not because tithing was never monetary. It was always agricultural to support the Levites. Secondly however, tithing teachers miss a major point. Jesus had not gone to the cross yet! Tithing was still in effect for Israel! No one is making the argument that tithing never existed! So even if you somehow can convince yourself that He was "teaching tithing" it is absurd to carry that over into New Testament giving. At best it was reinforcing the old Levitical model, which always was agriculture.

There are important lessons to be learned here though. Look at what is important to God. Is it money? Does Jesus accuse them of robbing God? He does tell them they should have tithed because the system was still intact but the point of this discourse is not to reinforce tithing. It was to reinforce the weightier matters. The things that matter more. Justice, mercy, and faithfulness. The vivid illustration He gives compares swallowing a camel to strain out a gnat! What is the gnat in this analogy beloved? Tithing! A gnat is an annoyance. A pest. It is the smaller picture. It is what matters less. The larger picture deals with the heart of God and is reinforced throughout Scripture:

Micah 6:8 Updated American Standard Version (UASV)

[8] He has told you, O man, what is good;
    and what does Jehovah require of you
but to do justice, and to love kindness,
    and to walk humbly with your God?

James 1:26-27 Updated American Standard Version (UASV)

[26] If any man thinks he is religious and does not bridle his tongue but deceives his heart, this person's religion is worthless. [27] Pure and undefiled

religion before[105] our God and Father is this: to visit orphans and widows in their affliction, and to keep oneself unstained by the world.

Here we have a Scripture from the Old Testament and one from the New Testament. The Micah Scripture says what is required of us by the Lord. No mention of tithing or giving. We are to do justice in this world. We are to not only be merciful, but we are to love mercy. We are to walk humbly before our God. How many times have we seen abusive tithing teachers fail in all three areas? Many preach that you have to tithe to them before paying your bills. How is that doing justly? Many leaders strip memberships for tithing infractions without consultation or trying to understand the individual circumstances. How is that loving mercy? Humility? I have heard leaders say that it is not your concern what he does with your money; your job is just to give it to him! It is very difficult to impossible to do as the Lord requires while enforcing a mandatory payment structure upon the sheep of God.

The James verses are even more interesting. Here we are provided with a contrast of worthless religion versus pure and undefiled religion. It seems in recent days it has become in vogue to bash the word religion. We need to be careful to call unclean what God has ordained. It is God who wrote the Bible. Religion is His word, not man's. To make the point, James compares good and bad religion. The person who cannot control his tongue and instead deceives his heart has a worthless religion. This may as well have been written about tithing teachers! While some are clearly aware of their lies, many are not. They are deceived because this is how they were taught. This is how we have always done it so we will continue to, even in the light of Scriptural revelation to the contrary. On the flip side, however, is pure and undefiled religion. To take care of the neediest in society; visiting widows and orphans in their affliction. I have heard tithing teachers say that you are not allowed to give your money to anyone in need until you have tithed correctly. In fact, most who teach tithing would probably agree with that. Widows and orphans? Not until you pay into the building fund! We think God is pleased with that? The second thing that makes religion pure and undefiled is to keep oneself from being stained by the world. One cannot argue that one of the greatest stains of the world the devil uses is money. It is ironic how often tithing teachers rebuke the sheep for not serving God and money while they are taking the offering from them! The hypocrisy is evident for those willing to see. The rich young ruler went away sad because money was more important to him than God and many leaders today exhibit the same sin. Mark Driscoll of Mars Hill Church

---

[105] Or *in the sight of*

in Seattle was recently caught stealing over $200,000 in tithe monies to pay a company to rig the NY Times Bestseller List system and ensure he ended up on the list. This potentially earned him over one million dollars personally. To date, he has yet to apologize, take ownership, or even admit that taking the tithe money for this was wrong. A church in Alabama recently spent tens of millions of dollars to build seven recreation domes as part of their facilities including a bowling alley. The pastor explained that it was to reach the lost. The Gospel? Not good enough anymore. Let's build a bowling alley. Undefiled by the stain of the world? No beloved. The truth is that so many churches today are running to embrace the world and leading the way down that path is a love for money fueled by the tithing deception.

So, did Jesus teach tithing? Absolutely not. The point He was making was not about tithing but rather about more important matters. He used tithing as an example to show how misguided the Pharisees were for obsessing about tithes while devouring widows' homes. We see the same thing today. Pastors owning multiple airplanes and living in multi-million-dollar mansions they actually call "parsonages" to avoid paying any taxes. Collecting tithes and offerings from the poor while they live the lifestyle of the rich and famous. Is there any justice, mercy or humility in that? Even if somehow you refuse to see the truth about why Jesus even mentioned tithing here you cannot avoid the fact that it still was agriculture and not money. You cannot avoid the fact that He had not gone to the cross yet, so the Levitical tithing system was still in place. You cannot avoid the truth if you really care to find it.

CHAPTER EIGHT The Seed-Sower Lies

"I broke the back of poverty with the $1,000 seed. I broke the back of poverty with the $1,000 seed. Listen carefully, this is, this is, possibly, possibly the most critical seed that you have ever planted in your lifetime. Because there is an anointing. I heard double portion. Did I hear double portion yesterday? There is going to be a doubling of your wisdom in six months. We're going to come in agreement; this is not for everybody. Every harvest requires a seed. God never opens His hand, opens His windows until we open our hands. But listen carefully, I don't know where you are going to get it. But if you can't even faith in a $1,000 seed to sow, how can you ever be debt free? If you can't even call in seed, how could you call in a harvest? You have to work with your faith for the seed before you can call in the harvest. But the Holy Spirit is giving me faith for 1189 miracles in the next 30 minutes or so. 1189, now that's not all. But there is a strong anointing for 1189 miracles. I'm going to tell you the three that I believe you will feel a special faith to focus the $1,000 seed for." - Mike Murdock Daystar Shareathon - September 2004

I know it is silly superstition, but I sometimes want to believe there is a special room in hell waiting for Michael Murdock. In our discussions in this book, I have tried to be careful in delineating between the deceived tithing teachers and the frauds. Scripture supports such a delineation:

2 Timothy 3:12-13 Updated American Standard Version (UASV)

[12] Indeed, all who desire to live godly in Christ Jesus will be persecuted. [13] But evil men and impostors will progress from bad to worse, deceiving and being deceived.

We brushed past this Scripture earlier and now revisit it. Paul is teaching his protégé Timothy that there will be impostors. Some will be deceived. They will not realize themselves that what they are teaching is not aligned with the truth of Scripture. Some others will clearly be deceivers. People who know full well they are lying and are using God or the veneer of piety to profit personally. The Bible describes them:

2 Peter 2:1-3 Updated American Standard Version (UASV)

[2] But false prophets also arose among the people, just as there will also be false teachers among you, who will secretly introduce destructive heresies, even denying the Master who bought them, bringing swift destruction upon themselves. [2] Many will follow their acts of shameless

conduct,[106] and because of them the way of the truth will be spoken of abusively; ³ and in their greed they will exploit you with false words; their judgment from long ago is not idle, and their destruction is not asleep.

They will make merchandise of you. If this does not fit the bill for some of the false tithing and prosperity teachers, I do not know what does. Perhaps the New Living Translation will bring it even more into focus for us:

2 Peter 2:3 New Living Translation (NLT)

³ In their greed they will make up clever lies to get hold of your money. But God condemned them long ago, and their destruction will not be delayed.

They will make up clever lies to get a hold of your money. That may as well be on the business cards of people like Mike Murdock. People who perpetrate one of the biggest frauds in Christendom; the seed-sower lie. The essentials of the lie, as with the most insidious schemes of Satan, mixes some truth with damnable heresies. As outlined at the start of this book, we are bound by the universal principle of sowing and reaping. As we saw, if we sow to our flesh we reap destruction, and if we sow to our Spirit we reap eternal life. This principle does carry over into finances as well. If we tend to horde money we will tend to poverty Proverbs teaches us. Once again, we cannot serve two masters. God does not want our love for money, the root of all sorts of evil, to supplant our love for Him. What folks like Murdock do however is they take what is good, pure and holy and pervert it for their own greed and gain. That quote from the Daystar shareathon is accurate and is essentially the same message you always hear from Murdock on television. Let us count the lies, schemes, and distortions of the Word of God:

1) It always starts with an unverifiable personal anecdote. Murdock wants us to believe that he sowed a thousand-dollar seed once that broke some kind of season of poverty in his life. This sets the premise that we give money to get money. No, hustlers like Murdock always state that you can't "buy blessings from God," but they preach just the opposite.

2) Step two is to hype up the opportunity. This is possibly the most important and critical seed you have ever planted...until the next shareathon of course. He has related to them and now hyped up what he is asking for.

---

[106] Or *their sensuality; their licentious ways; their brazen conduct*

3) Bathe the lies in pious sound religious gobbledygook. Because there's an anointing! Did I hear double portion! This is so shallow yet effective. People want to believe and if we do not do the work to show ourselves approved we can fall easily for such nonsense. The term anointing has been so abused in these last days there are few who truly understand its meaning. The word is biblical. It comes from the process of pouring oil on the head, such as was done with King Saul and then King David. It also can be rubbed in during a time of healing. David referred to Saul as God's anointed. So there is no question of the authenticity of the term. The problem is now how it is being used. I have seen it used to drive a wedge of superiority between the average congregant and the leader. That they are the chosen anointed of God and you are the miserable serf that is bound to follow them and bow down to their "authority." I have heard it used to describe gifted preachers - "my pastor is so anointed." I have heard it used to describe entire churches - "the anointing is flowing in that building." I have heard it mangled to deflect any criticism of a leader - "touch not God's anointed!" I have heard it abused to infer that you can transfer it to others or have it transferred to you. Renowned heretic Bill Johnson believes you can visit the dead and suck up some residual anointing from the grave! I have heard the unbiblical notion that you can have a double portion of the anointing. Or that you need a fresh anointing. Or that someone operates under a new anointing. All of this is nonsense.

1 John teaches us that we are all anointed if we are in Christ. You cannot have a double portion of the Holy Spirit. You never would need a fresh portion of the Holy Spirit - as if He goes stale! I certainly would never want a new spirit because then by default it would be demonic. Beloved, do not fall for the false authority paradigm so many operate under. The pastoral role is first a servant. The role of every Christian is supposed to be servanthood in humility.

The point here is that Murdock has established a relationship with them and hyped up the product. Now he covers it with key Christian buzzwords that are not being used in a Scripturally correct manner and are used solely to lend credibility to the sale. He then translates the religious-speak into tangible benefits for the people he is trying to make merchandise of. You're going to see double wisdom in six months. It always has to be a long period of time, so there is more time for the suckered sheep to forget or more time to attribute the everyday occurrence to the "sown seed."

4) Knowing full well that few people can afford to send $1000, Murdock strives to make this a "reserved opportunity." You want to make sure you get in on it! If you remember the example I opened the book with, this was the pattern for Bishop McNatt as well. Remember he claimed God

told him only ten people were to sow the $300 seed! The night I witnessed him there were more than 10 yet he prayed anyway and took their money. Back to Murdock, we see - this isn't for everyone! Are you one of the lucky ones to "come in agreement" with him?

5) Next up we see the heart of the lie. Every harvest needs a seed. God never opens the windows of heaven, until we open our hands. In terms of farming, he is absolutely right. You cannot harvest if you do not plant. The problem is that this has nothing to do with God and nothing further to do with money. What is the implication here? Clearly, Murdock is selling the notion that God will provide a harvest of more money in return for your seed of money. I have seen renowned heretic Benny Hinn actually claim God is going to multiply your seed by a specific amount, calling it a "wealth transfer." Shameless charlatans they are, fleecing the flock of God for personal gain.

6) Continuing to realize how reluctant people will be to send him that much money, Murdock goes for the kill. Suddenly it is not just a matter of harvest. It is a matter of faith. Those who worry about not being able to afford it are guilty of sinning against the Lord by showing a lack of faith. How utterly disgusting. Realize this is not just one happenstance in 2004. This can be seen every single day on the majority of "Christian" programming, and it is preached in pulpits across this country. Untold millions have been fleeced in the name of Jesus.

7) Lastly, put a time limit on it. This special anointing will only last 30 minutes! God is giving me faith for 1189 miracles! So now it is not just a monetary payback he is promising. He is promising on behalf of God Almighty, 1189 miracles for the first 1189 people stupid or desperate enough to call in the next 30 minutes. Do you realize that if he achieves the goal, he set he will pull in $1,189,000 in half an hour? That does not take a special faith. It does not take a special anointing. It takes a special level of not fearing the Lord. It takes an unbeliever. No one with the indwelt Holy Spirit can rob the sheep of God so callously and indifferently; mangling His holy Word all the while.

Look back through Scripture, and you will not find people who gave to God in order to be blessed. God made Abram a rich man long before he was going to sacrifice Isaac. God did not want a slice of Abram's wealth. He wanted his faith. Isaac and Jacob were likewise rich without having to sow anything. Joseph prospered without any seed. I once saw an advertisement from a snake oil salesman selling a "Joseph anointing" for a $500 "gift." What kind of anointing is that? You're sold into slavery, thrown into prison for something you didn't do and forgotten by everyone for 13 years? Not only that but this whole seed sower heresy cheapens what we ought to value.

Matthew 6:19-21 Updated American Standard Version (UASV)

[19] "Do not store up for yourselves treasures on earth, where moth and rust destroy, and where thieves break in and steal. [20] But store up for yourselves treasures in heaven, where neither moth nor rust destroys, and where thieves do not break in or steal; [21] for where your treasure is, there your heart will be also.

This is one of the chief reasons the church today is so carnal. The things of this world are glorified to them by people who are supposed to glorify only Christ. Too much of the church today teaches, honors, and supports storing up treasures on earth. People used to ask me all the time if I thought God wanted us to be poor. My answer would always be a milquetoast, "well no." The more I study this though, the more I think that if the question on your heart is whether God wants us to be poor, then the answer is yes. If money is what dominates your thinking when it comes to the things of God, then the answer is yes. God is infinitely more concerned about our character than our comfort. He sent His only Son to die a humiliating and excruciating death in our place so do not think for one second that He really just wants us to be comfortable. People ask me in jest sometimes why God will not let them win the lottery. My answer is always because He knows what would happen if you did! The object is not to have money be the object. Are there some rich believers? Absolutely but I guarantee they do not worship their money. It is not just Mike Murdock beloved. He is just the most brazen poster child. Earlier this year Paula White sent out a newsletter to her followers with the following subject line:

JULY IS PROPHETICALLY DESIGNATED FOR VICTORY OVER ENEMIES FOR THOSE WHO ALIGN THEMSELVES WITH ME IN THIS SEASON! DO NOT HESITATE!"

Proclaiming that this is a season of victory for His people, White unashamedly lied through her teeth by declaring that God told her that a $229 "seed" sown into her wallet will be a "breakthrough seed" for the month of July. How did she come up with such an odd number? Well, it comes from 1Chronicles 22:9 of course!

1 Chronicles 22:9 Updated American Standard Version (UASV)

[9] Look, a son shall be born to you who shall be a man of rest, I will give him rest from all his surrounding enemies, for his name shall be Solomon, and I will give peace and quiet to Israel in his days.

If you are looking at this and wondering what it has to do with sending Paula White $229, give yourself a pat on the back for discernment! This verse of course has nothing to do with sending money to anyone. It is strip mining the Bible for a point where God promises rest from your enemies and falsely applying it for everyone to make some money. Look I can do it too!

2 Samuel 7:11 Updated American Standard Version (UASV)

¹¹ from the day that I appointed judges over my people Israel. And I will give you rest from all your enemies. Also, Jehovah has told you that Jehovah will make a house for you.

Now, why didn't Paula White use this verse? Because then she could only charge $7.11! This kind of nonsense goes on every day in the church with far too many sheep falling for it. As we saw with Murdoch, it has similar characteristics to be watchful for. First of all, it is usually the result of a direct revelation from God to the false prophet. Why? Because the Bible never supports deception, so they must lie and say that they heard it from God. Here is another portion from White's newsletter:

"As I went deeper in the Spirit the Lord revealed that before the breakthrough comes, certain things must be dealt with. Specifically, there must be a complete defeat of your enemies! I need to explain the importance of this to you, so do not let this email go unread,"

Uh-huh. As she went deeper in the Lord He revealed to her how to rob His own people? I do not think so. Secondly, there is always an offer appealing to our flesh:

"This Email Will Change Your Life! YOU are on the verge of complete breakthrough in every area of your life. Spiritually, Financially, and Relationally God has shown me that this is a season of victory for His people."

Well! Sign me up! Just like we saw in the Mike Murdock example. You must realize the sheer lunacy of this "prophecy." That EVERYONE is on the verge of complete and total breakthrough. Thirdly, just as we saw before, they throw a little Bible in it for show:

1 Chronicles 22:7-8 Updated American Standard Version (UASV)

⁷ David said to Solomon, "My son, I had it in my heart to build a house to the name of Jehovah my God. ⁸ But the word of Jehovah came to me, saying, 'You have shed much blood and have waged great wars. You shall not build a house to my name, because you have shed so much blood before me on the earth.

It is too bad she did not actually READ those Scriptures because they spell out in no uncertain terms that the reason David was denied building the temple was that he was a man of war who shed too much blood! There is no mention of his age! The false prophet however relies on your biblical ignorance. White continues that you "must know how to legally engage the enemy for his unconditional defeat" and that part of that legality involves "following prophetic instruction." The implication being that if you do not send her cash, you are being disobedient to the prophetic instruction you are receiving and are giving legal right to the enemy to run wild in your life. Sound familiar? That is the same model Murdock used when he started making it an issue of your faith! Again, I say, how disgusting.

Lastly, in this case, we see a form of numerology involved to make it appear more spiritual. Mike Murdoch once sold a Psalm 139 blessing if you sent him $139. It is usually pretty transparent. White at least realized that not everyone can afford $229 so she offers a knockoff version of this bogus prophecy. The newsletter says if you cannot produce the $229 seed then you should send her a $31 seed because there are 31 days in July and because 22 + 9 = 31. I kid you not. Yet despite the crass obvious nature of her falseness she still has over 1.7 million likes on Facebook. I see well-grounded Christians constantly repost her status every day. Do we understand what this means? Paul White is lying about hearing from God. She is lying about it in order to steal money from the people of God. I do not care if her next post is biblically accurate. We need to stop drawing people to her. She is a con artist and a charlatan who practices divination for money. Do not try and find excuses for her. Do not pass go. Do not collect $229. Still not convinced? Here is the body of the letter Benny Hinn sent regarding the wealth transfer:

"Your Double Harvest Miracle - Are you ready for God to do the "impossible" in your life! Are you ready to see your harvest doubled? Are you ready to see your debt cancelled in the next 90 days? Imagine not dreading going to the mailbox, no bills piling up on your counter, and no calls from collectors coming to your home. God wants to wipe your debt out! Every bit of it" and in the next 90 days! This is an appointed hour. Imagine: Your $100 gift immediately doubles to $200. Your $500 seed literally becomes $1,000. If God leads you to plant $10,000, it instantly grows into a $20,000 seed! And your double seed, sown bountifully, will reap bountifully through the supernatural law of multiplication! Only God could provide something like this--a double harvest for you. And the more you plant, the more you will reap! The anointing for biblical abundance is being released. As you step into this miracle by faith, it will be poured out upon you, too! Your giving is literally the weapon that breaks the bondage of debt in this ministry and in your home during the next 90 days. Plant

your seed-gift now, then begin confessing over every bill, every debt, and every area of financial struggle in your life: "With God I'm coming out of debt in 90 days!!!" These repeated confessions will be constant reminders of the financial breakthrough that is coming to you.

We see the same scheme. The same outline. Enough religiosity to make it feel pious. Playing to our fleshly desire for earthly gain. Insisting the timing has to be now. Benny, of course, is just as outrageous promising a double return on your seed. I think the point has been made. These examples are not outliers. They are the norm today for the seed sowing prosperity gospel that has enslaved so many. God is not holding back His blessings because you have not sown a seed. We must realize that while Hinn, White, and Murdock are the big names playing this scam on large levels, the same crime is perpetrated on the local level as well. Week in and week out tithing is often preached in this manner. That God wants to throw open the windows of heaven if only you would be obedient! There is no double harvest miracle. There is no $229 breakthrough seed. There is no $1000 uncommon seed. There are only those who know the truth of God's Word and those who submit to being fleeced.

CHAPTER NINE The Hebrews Confirms Tithing Lie

Only in the twisted, depraved mind of the tithing teacher can a chapter dedicated to bringing glory to Jesus as our new High Priest, be used as a defense of tithing. Yet that is exactly what we hear from the tithing advocates when they prop up the seventh chapter in the Book of Hebrews. We need to keep mind as we go through the verses the immediate context. Who is the author writing to? He is writing to the Messianic Jews who were still trying to mix law into their new-found grace. Let us go through the entire chapter:

Hebrews 7:1-3 Updated American Standard Version (UASV)

7 For this Melchizedek, king of Salem, priest of the Most High God, who met Abraham as he was returning from the slaughter of the kings and blessed him, ² to whom also Abraham apportioned a tenth part of all the spoils, was first of all, by the translation of his name, king of righteousness, and then also king of Salem, which is king of peace. ³ Without father, without mother, without genealogy, having neither beginning of days nor end of life, but made like the Son of God, he remains a priest forever.

The writer is trying to make the point to the messianic Jews that Jesus is now our High Priest. He starts by laying the groundwork on who Melchizedek was. The mention of a tithe, tenth, is first and foremost a restatement of historical fact. One the writer knew the Hebrews would know and understand. No one is arguing that Abram didn't give a tenth, one time, to this king and high priest. The argument ensues when you try to take a onetime event and create a universal principle out of thin air to try and rob the sheep of God. We continue:

Hebrews 7:4-10 Updated American Standard Version (UASV)

⁴ Now observe how great this man was to whom Abraham, the patriarch, gave a tenth of the choicest spoils. ⁵ And those indeed of the sons of Levi who receive the priest's office have commandment in the Law to collect [b]a tenth from the people, that is, from their brothers, although these are descended from Abraham. ⁶ But this man who does not have his descent from them received tithes from Abraham and blessed the one who had the promises. ⁷ It is beyond dispute that the inferior is blessed by the superior. ⁸ In the one case tithes are received by mortal men, but in the other case, by one of whom it is testified that he lives. ⁹ And, so to speak,

through Abraham even Levi, who received tithes, paid tithes, ¹⁰ for he was still in the loins of his forefather when Melchizedek met him.

Melchizedek is what is known as a type of Christ. As he was the high priest in the days of Abram, as Jesus is our High Priest today. The writer here though realizes he must convey that the superiority of Christ to the Levitical priests whom the Hebrews would currently esteem. Thomas D. Lea comments on these verses as follows:

> **7:4.** This verse repeats his emphasis on Melchizedek's greatness, this strange priest-king from Salem. No one could dispute the greatness of Abraham. Jews saw him as the father of Israel. Christians saw him as the "father of all who believe" (Rom. 4:11). The writer of Hebrews designated Abraham as **the patriarch.** In the original language the word for "patriarch" ended the verse, a position of emphasis. The text declares, "It was our patriarch Abraham himself who gave the tithe." The great Abraham gave his tithe to the even greater Melchizedek.
>
> **7:5–6a.** The Law provided that the people should pay tithes to the Levites (Num. 18:21, 24). The Levites paid tithes to the priests, so that we could actually say that the people paid tithes to the priests (Num. 18:26–32). The people who paid the tithes in the Old Testament and the priests who received them were **brothers.** The priests receiving the tithes were not superior to the payees. They were kin to them. Their ability to collect tithes did not come from any inherent superiority but from the commandment in the Law.
>
> Melchizedek, however, was different. He did not receive tithes from any special commandment in the Law but from his inherent superiority. Abraham's spontaneous action implied Melchizedek's superiority.
>
> Melchizedek did not trace his lineage from Levi. He was not a brother to the Levites. He stood out as a lonely figure of grandeur. He did not receive tithes from his brothers, but from Abraham. Abraham's willing surrender of a tenth of his spoils to Melchizedek further revealed the majesty of this mysterious priest.
>
> **7:6b–7.** Melchizedek not only received tithes from Abraham, but he also blessed the patriarch. The act of blessing showed the acceptance of the implied superiority. Anyone who read the account in the Old Testament would see this principle without additional explanation. Abraham acknowledged the greatness of Melchizedek by accepting the blessing from him. Jewish readers would perceive that **the lesser person is blessed by the greater.**

7:8. This verse draws from the silence of Scripture to undergird Melchizedek's greatness. The Levitical priesthood is contrasted with the priesthood of Melchizedek. The Old Testament priests were mortal men. After a few years of service to God, they would die. Melchizedek, however, served in a priesthood which enjoyed a continual existence. Records show the death of generation after generation of Levitical priests, but not of Melchizedek. Levites transferred their position and duties to their heirs. Israelites paid tithes to these mortals. Abraham paid his tithes to one whom Scripture never showed to be anything except a living person. Scripture's silence could thus be seen as a type representing the eternal priesthood of Christ.

Hebrews will show that Jesus lived forever by his statements in 7:16, 24. The Bible recorded that Christ died and rose again from the dead. He is now alive for eternity. The doctrine is made practical with the observations of 7:23–25.

7:9–10. One final piece of evidence testifies to the superiority of Melchizedek to that of the Levitical priests. In one sense we might say that even Levi paid tithes to Melchizedek. The writer of Hebrews prepared his readers that his argument would take an unusual twist with his statement, **One might even say**. It is almost as if he said, "Do not press this too literally." His argument would carry more force to a Jew familiar with the concept of solidarity or unity of purpose and interest than to a twentieth-century American emphasizing individuality. The idea is that neither the father nor the children would be independent of one another. Levi here is more than an individual. He served as ancestor and representative of the Jewish priesthood.

Since Levi was Abraham's great-grandson and was unborn when Abraham met Melchizedek, he could be described as already in Abraham's loins. Biblical thought accepted the idea that an ancestor contained within himself all of his descendants.

Although Levi had not yet been born when Abraham paid the tithes, we could view him as paying tithes to Melchizedek by this manner of reckoning. The payment of tithes by Abraham could be transferred to his offspring Levi and to all the priesthood. If we view the statement from the standpoint of solidarity, the payment of tithes by Levi through Abraham becomes more evident than Levi's right to receive tithes from others. If Levi paid the tithes to Melchizedek, this demonstrates even more clearly the superiority of Melchizedek.

> In these seven verses are listed four evidences of the greatness of the priesthood of Melchizedek:
>
> 1. Abraham gave him tithes.
> 2. Melchizedek blessed Abraham.
> 3. Melchizedek had an eternal priesthood.
> 4. Levi paid tithes to Melchizedek through Abraham.[107]

David L. Allen takes a deeper look at these verses,

> **7:4** Hebrews 7:4–10 is a self-contained paragraph unit in which the author further theologizes about Melchizedek.[108] Louw and Nida wrongly take the verb *theōreite*, translated "just think," as an indicative.[109] It is better taken as an imperative as do virtually all commentators and all translations with the exception of the TEV. The word translated "how great" is used by the author as a term of exclamation, and coupled with the imperative verb is an attention getter: "see (just think, consider, notice) how great he is (was)!" The demonstrative pronoun "this one," translated "he," must have an equative verb supplied to finish out the meaning in English. Translators and commentators are about evenly divided in favor of the present or past tense of the verb to be supplied. Contextually, either is permissible.
>
> The greatness of Melchizedek is defined by the author in the next statement: "Even the patriarch Abraham gave him a tenth of the plunder!" Two words in this clause are emphatic by their position: "tenth," which is fronted in the clause before the subject and verb, and "the patriarch," which is placed last in the clause to emphasize further the greatness of Melchizedek. The use of the definite article further suggests Melchizedek's greatness.[110] The word translated "plunder" may signal that Abraham gave not only a tenth of the spoils taken in his victory over the kings, but the choicest or best of the spoils.[111]

---

[107] Thomas D. Lea, *Hebrews, James*, vol. 10, Holman New Testament Commentary (Nashville, TN: Broadman & Holman Publishers, 1999), 130–132.

[108] Westfall, *Discourse Analysis*, 182, views Heb 7:4–28 as "the deferred answer to the questions that are raised by 2:5–18 and 5:1–10."

[109] L&N 32.11. They correctly note that the semantic domain of this verb is "come to understand" and that semantically the dominant meaning of such verbs has to do with the process by which one arrives at understanding.

[110] Hughes, *Hebrews*, 251.

[111] Lane, *Hebrews 1–8*, 168.

7:5 The *men ... de* construction in Greek at the beginning of vv. 5, 6 ties them together in the sense of "on the one hand [v. 5] ... on the other hand [v. 6]." Verse 5 functions as an explanatory statement giving the ground or reason for the collection of the tithe by the Levites. The ground for such an action is the Mosaic law, specifically given in Num 18:21-24. Those decedents of Levi who have "received" the priestly office (the Greek implies they received this office from God) are responsible for the collection of the tithe. This "commandment" that the priests have received concerning the tithe is "according to the law."[112] Lane caught the important nuance from the author's identification of the "people" as "brothers," namely, those who received the tithes (sons of Levi) and those who gave them (the people of Israel) are all Abraham's descendants and are treated by the author as equals. It was Abraham from whom both groups, Levitical priests and all the people, sprang; and it was Abraham, great as he was, who recognized the claim of Melchizedek, one even greater than Abraham, to receive a tithe. From this the author concludes in vv. 9-10 that Melchizedek is superior to the Levitical priests, hence his priesthood is superior to that of the Levitical line.[113]

7:6 Friberg and Friberg give the introductory *de* of v. 6 a hyperordinating tag, which semantically signals the information in v. 6 is more prominent than v. 5.[114] The present tense participle with the negative ("did not trace his descent") indicates customary action[115] in the sense that Melchizedek regularly does not have his genealogy traced from Levi. The participle is attributive by virtue of the definite article, but it functions concessively, as expressed with "however ... yet," where the two verbs "collected" and "blessed" express contraexpectation. Melchizedek did two things that Levitical priests do: he collected a tithe, and he blessed Abraham. Yet the author's point is that Melchizedek himself was not descended from Levi. Not only that, he was not descended from Abraham either, but was Abraham's contemporary in time and superior in rank. As the recipient of the blessing, Abraham is in

---

[112] The phrase κατὰ τὸν νόμον, "according to the Law," can be connected with "to collect a tenth from the people," but it is better to connect it with ἐντολὴν ἔχουσιν, "they have a commandment." The NIV conflates the specific word ἐντολὴν into the more general word νόμος in keeping with the Hebrew notion that the latter is the sum of all the commandments. The word used in this verse for collecting tithes is used in the same manner in the LXX in 1 Sam 8:15, 17 and Neh 10:37.

[113] Lane, *Hebrews 1-8*, 168-69.[113]

[114] D. Friberg and B. Friberg, *Analytical Greek New Testament* (Grand Rapids: Baker, 1981), 671.

[115] Alford, "Hebrews," 133.

an inferior position to the one who gave the blessing. The use of the perfect tense "blessed him" indicates the superiority of Melchizedek, the ongoing relevance of the action from the author's perspective, and the permanent status of Melchizedek as superior to Abraham.[116] Abraham is described as "him who had the promises," harking back to the discussion in Heb 6:13–20. Nothing else is said about the "promises," indicating the meaning would be clear to the readers. We have seen how important the concept of "promise" is to the author; God is the author of the promises to Abraham, through whom Christ would come and fulfill them all. This is the theological trajectory of the author in Heb 7:1–10:18.

7:7 In v. 7, the author parenthetically draws the lesser-greater distinction by pointing out that "without doubt"[117] the lesser person, Abraham, is blessed by the greater, Melchizedek. The "lesser person" indicates a person with lesser status; the "greater" indicates a person of greater status, prominence, or rank. The inferior is blessed by the superior. Abraham is only "inferior" to Melchizedek in terms of rank or status. Both words "lesser" and "greater" are articular and in the neuter gender in Greek, where the article focuses on the qualities indicated by the words,[118] and the neuter gender serves to generalize the reference.[119]

7:8 New information is added to the argument in v. 8 with the assertion that the collection of the tithe under Mosaic law was made by Levitical priests who die. However, in the case of Melchizedek, the tithe is collected by one "who is declared to be living." This contrast is made all the more emphatic by the Greek construction. Levites are mortals, but it is said of Melchizedek that he is "declared" to be living. The Levites are dying men (the participle[120] precedes the noun in Greek to emphasize mortality) who receive tithes; Melchizedek is one who, typologically declared to be living, received a tithe from Abraham. The obvious result of the death of the Levitical priests is that the priesthood is left to another person. This harks back to 7:3 and to the argument from silence made there concerning any lack of information historically about

---

[116] See Bruce, *Hebrews*, 162–163; Lane, *Hebrews 1–8*, 169; and Ellingworth, *Hebrews*, 365–66.

[117] The phrase in Greek means "without contradiction, question, doubt." The author's statement is one with which everyone would agree.

[118] Greenlee, *Exegetical Summary*, 238; Lane, *Hebrews 1–8*, 158.[118]

[119] Attridge, *Hebrews*, 196.

[120] The participle functions attributively describing "men" and can be so without the article since the noun it modifies, ἄνθρωποι, is anarthrous as well (Greenlee, *Exegetical Summary*, 239). The present tense is "frequentative," describing action that recurs from time to time (Lane, *Hebrews 1–8*, 158). Some translators (NASB) and commentators (Bruce, *Hebrews*, 161; and Lane, *Hebrews 1–8*, 158–59) give it an adjectival translation: "mortal men."[120]

Melchizedek's death. The text does not say that Melchizedek is living, but is "declared"[121] to be living. It is Scripture that bears this testimony, specifically the author's juxtaposition of Gen 14:17–20 with Ps 110:4. The author is still moving in a typological milieu. Bruce captures the intent well: "The tithe which Abraham gave to Melchizedek was received by one who, as far as the record goes, has no 'end of life.'"[122]

7:9–10 The section is concluded in vv. 9–10, a single sentence in Greek. The idiomatic expression translated "one might even say" in v. 9 leads to the author's concluding point in the comparison of Melchizedek and Levi with respect to the tithe. "One might even say" implies a certain "conscious literary license" on the part of the author indicating he was not speaking "literally" of Levi being in Abraham's loins. This provides another indication that the overall tenor of Heb 7:1–10 is typological in nature, and not an attempt by the author to affirm any divine status on Melchizedek. The author deftly makes the point by playing on the noun translated "tenth" and the verb translated "collect," the same root word in Greek used first as an active participle ("who collects the tenth") then as a perfect passive verb. The meaning could be rendered "One might even say that Levi, who collects the tithe, was through Abraham 'tithed' or 'collected from' by Melchizedek." Abraham, as a representative of all his descendents, including Levi, by means of the concept of corporate solidarity, contained in his body the seed of all his offspring. Levi, who centuries later would receive tithes from the people, paid tithes to Melchizedek through Abraham, since he was considered by the author to be "still in the body of his ancestor." For the author of Hebrews, since Levi was reckoned as still in the body of his ancestor, actions taken by Abraham were actions taken by Levi as well.

The author has now completed his purpose in Heb 7:4–10 by showing why the Melchizedekian priesthood is superior to the Levitical priesthood. From his own exegetical treatment of Gen 14:17–20, the author has made his case for the superiority of the Melchizedekian priesthood over the Levitical priesthood because the Levites paid tithes to Melchizedek while still in the "loins" of Abraham. In one fell theological swoop, the author subordinates the entire Levitical priesthood to Melchizedek. Building on this point, the author shifts the

---

[121] The use of the Greek present passive participle of μαρτυρέω, "to be testified" or "to have witness borne," indicates it is Scripture that is bearing this ongoing testimony. Gieschen's assessment (*Angelomorphic Christology*, 310) may be correct that the testimony is not that of the silence of Gen 14, but the testimony of Ps 110:4 as it was interpreted by the author.[121]

[122] Bruce, *Hebrews*, 163.

> focus of the argument from Melchizedek to the Levitical priests in Heb 7:11–19, and from there he makes the shift to Christ in Heb 7:20–28.[123]
>
> Melchizedek has become for the author a "type" of Christ in the sense of the timeless nature of his priestly office without successor. The author builds on the historical account of Melchizedek in Genesis 14, but his argument is "thoroughly Christological." Lane concluded: "Accordingly, christology, and not speculation, is the determining factor in the portrayal of Melchizedek in 7:1–10."[124]

Do we see any focus on the mention of the word tithe or tenth? Any focus at all on money? Of course, not because that is not what this chapter is about. It is however how tithing teachers operate. They find any mention of the word, ignore the context and purpose of using the word, and add it to their theology as proof.

Hebrews 7: 11-14 Updated American Standard Version (UASV)

11 Now if perfection had been attainable through the Levitical priesthood (for under it the people received the law), what further need would there have been for another priest to arise after the order of Melchizedek, and not according to the order of Aaron? 12 For when the priesthood changes, of necessity there is a change of the law also. 13 For the one of whom these things are spoken belonged to another tribe, from which no one has officiated at the altar. 14 For it is evident that our Lord was descended from Judah, a tribe with reference to which Moses spoke nothing concerning priests.

Pay close attention here to these verses. The shameless audacity to claim Hebrews 7 as supporting tithing is beyond the pale because this group of verses does away with the priesthood and the laws which governed it. These verses actually prove the elimination of tithing as a practice! Do we remember what happened when Jesus died?

Matthew 27:50-51 Updated American Standard Version (UASV)

50 And Jesus cried out again with a loud voice and yielded up his spirit.[125] 51 And look, the curtain of the temple was torn in two, from top to bottom; and the earth shook, and the rocks were split. 52 The tombs

---

[123] Joslin, "Theology of the Mosaic Law in Hebrews 7:1–10:18," 178.[123]

[124] David L. Allen, *Hebrews*, The New American Commentary (Nashville, TN: B & H Publishing Group, 2010), 415–418.

[125] I.e. the life-force (life-giving breath; breath of life); Jesus gave up his life, he died

also were opened, and many bodies of the holy ones who had fallen asleep were raised;

The veil of the temple is what kept the people out from the Holy of Holies. Jesus tore the veil and reconciled us to God. Thus the Levitical priesthood is no longer necessary, and tithing only existed because of the need to provide for the Levitical priests. When there is a change in the priesthood, there is a change in the law as well! What is the change? The Priest now comes from the Tribe of Judah, not Levi. He is the Lion of the Tribe of Judah. He is the Christ. He does not require tithes as the Levitical priests did. To use Hebrews 7 to try and justify tithing is patently silly and requires you to dismiss the entire chapter for the fact that the word "tithe" merely appears in the historical narrative.

Hebrews 7:15-19 Updated American Standard Version (UASV)

15 And this becomes even clearer when another priest arises according to the likeness of Melchizedek, 16 who has become a priest not according to a law of physical requirement, but according to the power of an indestructible life. 17 For it is witnessed of him,

"You are a priest forever, according to the order of Melchizedek."[126]

18 For, on the one hand, there is a setting aside of a former commandment because of its weakness and uselessness 19 (for the Law made nothing perfect), and on the other hand there is a bringing in of a better hope, through which we draw near to God.

The Old Testament priests were chosen based upon a legal requirement concerning the tribe they originated from. Jesus however fills the office based upon the power of an indestructible life. By defeating the grave! He is our Priest forever beloved! The key here though is in verse 18:

For on the one hand, a former commandment is set aside because of its weakness and uselessness

The commandment that is laid aside is the Levitical system entirely. It is removed entirely for our new High Priest. Commentators agree. Thomas D. Lea states:

> **7:18–19.** Verse 18 shows the weakness of the Law, while verse 19 describes the new hope which Christ's priesthood provides. Verse 18 makes three statements about the Law and the priesthood connected with it: (1) weak, (2) useless, (3) annulled. The Law provided a standard

---

[126] A quotation from Ps 110:4

> by which a person could evaluate moral condition, but in its weakness it could not provide life and spiritual vigor to anyone. It was merely a diagnostic tool. It was useless because it could not provide a constant means of access to God. These two deficiencies made it necessary to set the Law aside.
>
> This does not mean that the Law was annulled in that it no longer had any use. It served the function of revealing sin (Rom. 3:20), but it could not bring perfection. It could only demonstrate imperfection. It reminded sinners of their sin. The establishment of a new priesthood meant that the old Levitical priesthood no longer had divine authority. A new priesthood which could give power over sin had come into operation.
>
> Verse 19 introduces a theme of hope (cf. 6:19). The hope Christ provided was better than the empty regulations of the Levitical priesthood and the commandments which produced it. Christ's priesthood made it possible for sinners to **draw near to God** (see 10:22 and often in Hebrews).
>
> Wandering sinners seeking for God find much hope in Hebrews. The new priesthood of Melchizedek provided a foundation for such optimism. Believers can draw near to God even though **God is a consuming fire** (Heb. 12:29). Seekers can actually find God.[127]

The nature and order of Christ do not require the tithing system the Levite required. Verse 18 officially replaces the entire Levitical priest system with Jesus Christ as our new High Priest. The new regulation is grace, not law. Tithing is forever abolished. In fact, a preacher who promotes tithing in light of these truths promotes the law over grace. They promote that which could not make anything perfect in place of He who can perfect us through His blood.

And it was not without an oath. For those who formerly became priests were made such without an oath, but this one was made a priest with an oath by the one who said to him:

Hebrews 7:20-21 Updated American Standard Version (UASV)

[20] And inasmuch as it was not without an oath [21] (for they indeed became priests without an oath, but he with an oath through the one who said to him,

"The Lord has sworn and will not change his mind, 'You are a priest forever;'")

---

[127] Thomas D. Lea, *Hebrews, James*, vol. 10, Holman New Testament Commentary (Nashville, TN: Broadman & Holman Publishers, 1999), 135.

The oath referred to here was outlined in the previous chapter:

Hebrews 6:17-20 Updated American Standard Version (UASV)

17 In the same way God, wanting to show even more to the heirs of the promise the unchangeableness of his resolve, guaranteed it with an oath, 18 so that by two unchangeable things, in which it is impossible for God to lie, we who have fled for refuge might have strong encouragement to hold fast to the hope set before us; 19 which we have like an anchor of the soul, both firm and steadfast, and entering into the inside of the curtain, 20 where Jesus has entered as a forerunner for us, having become a high priest forever according to the order of Melchizedek.

Beloved, there will be no need for a change again. The law failed to produce the desired effect for God but His Son did not, cannot, and will never fail. We have that oath from God and God can never lie. God will not change His mind! Jesus Christ is our Priest forever! Hallelujah to the Lamb!

Hebrews 7:22-25 Updated American Standard Version (UASV)

22 so much the more also Jesus has become the guarantee of a better covenant.

23 And indeed many have become priests, because they were prevented by death from continuing, 24 but he, because he continues forever, holds the priesthood permanently. 25 Therefore He is able also to save forever those who draw near to God through him, since he always lives to make intercession for them.

I so wish that tithing preachers would really wrap their spirit around this. Jesus personally guarantees a better covenant than the one that included tithing. When they try and enforce tithing they are in fact choosing the failed old covenant over Christ. Even within the Levitical portions of the covenant, it was always limited because the priests were limited. They were human. They would live and die. Jesus however lives forever. There are no limitations in Christ. The comparison made here is striking. Under the Levitical system, only the priests could draw near to God. Now through Christ, who always lives to make intercession for us, we all can draw near to God. Why in the world would any minister of the Gospel preach a system that divides people away from Jesus when they can draw near? Going back to the text, Hebrews 7 concludes:

Hebrews 7:26-28 Updated American Standard Version (UASV)

26 For it is fitting for us to have such a high priest who is loyal, innocent, undefiled, separated from the sinners,[128] and exalted above the

---

[128] **Sinner:** (*hamartōlos*) In the Scriptures "sinners" is generally used in a more specific way, that is, referring to those willfully living in sin, practicing sin, or have a reputation of

heavens. [27] He has no need, like those high priests, to offer sacrifices daily, first for his own sins and then for those of the people, since he did this once for all when he offered up himself. [28] For the law appoints men as high priests who have weakness, but the statement of the oath, after the law, appoints a Son, who is made perfect forever.

What powerful verses for us as believers. The cross accomplished what the Levitical system and the law never could. The cross was the final sacrifice. The one that removed our sins permanently. There is no more need for the Levitical system because the cross destroyed it. This is not some fly by night capricious hope beloved. This is promised by oath from Almighty God. Think for a moment however how important Hebrews 7 is in our doctrine. The establishment of Jesus Christ as our High Priest. He destroyed the law and nailed it to the cross. He tore the veil that separated us from God. He replaced the Levitical priests and made intercession for us forevermore. Restoring us to God. To take this importance and cheapen it to try and steal money from people is quite egregious. I pray those who continue to teach such heresy repent soon. Tomorrow is promised to no one.

---

sinning. – Matt. 9:10; Mark 2:15; Luke 5:30; 7:37-39; John 9:16; Rom. 3:7; Gal. 2:15; 1 Tim. 1:15; Heb. 7:26; Jam. 4:8; 1 Pet 4:18; Jude 1:15.

CHAPTER TEN The First Fruits Lie

As we have seen, tithing teachers will stop at nothing to create whole doctrine out of thin air. Cobbling together stories and verse fragments to pretend that God has always demanded tithing and thus nothing has changed today. One of the more recent deceptions I came across was the erroneous teaching that tithing is actually part of a larger biblical principle of first fruits. This came to my attention when I saw renowned heretic Perry Noble preach an abusive tithing message this year. Noble hit all of the usual heresies we have already reviewed including the Abram, Jacob, Hebrews, and "Jesus taught tithing" lies. He started however with the notion that tithing started as a principle of first fruits established in Genesis 4 in the story of the sacrifices offered by Cain and Abel. Noble gleefully says that Cain brought "some" but Abel brought the first fruits. Therefore, he concludes - the principle is established so you have to bring him your first fruits as well. Let's take a look at what God's Word actually says:

Genesis 4:3-7 Updated American Standard Version (UASV)

3 And in the course of time[129] Cain brought to Jehovah an offering of the fruit of the ground. 4 And Abel, he also brought of the firstlings of his flock and of their fat portions. And Jehovah had regard for Abel and his offering; 5 but for Cain and his offering he had no regard. So Cain was very angry, and his face fell.[130] 6 Then Jehovah said to Cain, "Why are you angry, and why has your face fallen? 7 If you do well, will there not be a lifting up?[131] And if you do not do well, sin is crouching at the door. Its desire is for you, but you must rule over it."

Beloved, this is what I mean when I say you do not create doctrine out of thin air. If the Bible does not expressly state why something happened we are not free to guess. These verses in no way state *why* God was displeased with the offering of Cain. Frankly, the usage of the term, "Abel *also* brought of the firstborn" might indicate that the Cain offering was first fruits as well! Now Hebrews 11 tells us that Abel's sacrifice was more excellent but again the "why" is missing. That brings us to one last verse regarding this story:

---

[129] Lit., *of days*
[130] Or, his countenance fell
[131] This is a shortening of the Hebrew idiom "to lift up the face," which means "to accept" favorably

1 John 3:11-12 Updated American Standard Version (UASV)

[11] For this is the message which you have heard from the beginning, that we should love one another; [12] not as Cain, who was of the evil one and violently slaughtered his brother. And for what reason did he slaughter him? Because his deeds were evil, and the ones of his brother were righteous.

God is clearly making a distinction not of the type of sacrifice but rather of the condition of the heart of the one making the offering. Cain was evil, and Abel was righteous. Either way, to take the expression "firstborn of the flock" and create doctrine out of it is not only poor theology - it is false theology. And Noble goes farther than that! He claims that this establishes a principle! Well, if by principle he meant that God honors righteousness and abhors evil then yes. That is not what Noble is preaching here though. He is claiming that this one expression lasting all of four words establishes a bedrock principle that says you have to give him 10% of your income. That is ridiculous. Moving past the misuse of Cain and Abel, there are plenty of Scriptures that actually speak about first fruits. Let us examine what first fruits were intended to be in the Old Testament and how the term is used under the New Covenant.

Leviticus 23:9-14 Updated American Standard Version (UASV)

[9] And Jehovah spoke to Moses, saying, [10] "Speak to the sons of Israel and say to them, 'When you come into the land that I give you and reap its harvest, you shall bring the sheaf of the firstfruits of your harvest to the priest. [11] And he shall wave the sheaf before Jehovah, so that you may be accepted; on the day after the sabbath the priest shall wave it. [12] And on the day when you wave the sheaf, you shall offer a male lamb a year old without blemish as a burnt offering to Jehovah. [13] And the grain offering with it shall be two tenths of an ephah[132] of fine flour mixed with oil, a food offering to Jehovah with a pleasing aroma, and the drink offering with it shall be of wine, a fourth of a hin.[133] [14] And you shall eat neither bread nor grain parched or fresh until this same day, until you have brought the offering of your God. It is a statute forever throughout your generations in all your dwellings.

This is the establishment of first fruits. Unlike Perry Noble seems to think it was not a universal principle established during the time of Cain and Abel. It was one of the feasts created by the Lord as part of the Mosaic Law. It is a feast of remembrance for the Israelites. To remember their bondage in slavery and how the Lord delivered them from Egypt. It also

---

[132] Two tenths of an ephah equaled 4.4 L (4 dry qt).
[133] A hin equaled 3.67 L (7.75 pt).

started the clock for counting the time for the feast of weeks. Israel was an agrarian society. It was organized based upon the growth of the crops it raised. There is no principle here about money, which the Israelites possessed at this time as well. This is not a principle about wealth or increase or anything portending blessings in the future. It was a way of remembering the past. Of all God had already done. There is a lesson there for the greedy money chasers of today who keep trying to make blessings to be about things we have not received as opposed to all God has already done. We move on to Deuteronomy.

Deuteronomy 26:1-11 Updated American Standard Version (UASV)

26 "And it shall be, when you come into the land that Jehovah your God gives you as an inheritance, and you possess it and live in it, **2** that you shall take of the first of all the fruit of the ground, which you shall bring in from your land that Jehovah your God gives you; and you shal put it in a basket, and shall go to the place where Jehovah your God shall choose, to make his name to dwell there. **3** And you shall come to the priest who is in office in those days, and say to him, 'I declare this day to Jehovah your God, that I have entered the land which Jehovah swore to our fathers to give us. **4** Then the priest shall take the basket from your hand and set it down before the altar of Jehovah your God. **5** "And you shall make response before Jehovah your God, 'A wandering Aramean[134] was my father. And he went down into Egypt and sojourned there, few in number, and there he became a nation, great, mighty, and populous. **6** And the Egyptians treated us harshly and afflicted us and laid on us hard labor. **7** Then we cried to Jehovah, the God of our fathers, and Jehovah heard our voice and saw our affliction, our toil, and our oppression; **8** and Jehovah brought us out of Egypt with a mighty hand and an outstretched arm and with great terror and with signs and wonders; **9** and he has brought us to this place and has given us this land, a land flowing with milk and honey. **10** Now behold, I have brought the first of the produce of the ground which you, O Jehovah have given me.' And you shall set it down before Jehovah your God, and worship before Jehovah your God; **11** and you shall rejoice in all the good that the Lord your God has given to you

---

[134] **Aram; Aramaeans:** (Heb. *arămmî*) These were the descendants of Shem's son Aram, who mainly lived in various regions N of Israel, running from the Lebanon Mountains across to Mesopotamia and from the Taurus Mountains in the north down to Damascus. The Aramaeans hardly ever formed any kind of nation state; rather they lived as self-governing, autonomous towns and tribes settled by nomads before 1000 B.C.E. However, if they were threatened, they were quick to form alliances with neighboring towns of Aramaeans and even other countries. However, once the threat was over, they went back to their independence, fighting amongst themselves. The area known as Aram in Hebrew would later be referred to as Syria, and its people as the Syrians.—Gen. 25:20; Deut. 26:5; Hos 12:12.

and to your house, you, and the Levite, and the foreign resident who is among you.

Now, remember, the false teachers and prophets want you to believe that God has established a principle of first fruits which now requires you to bring your tithe to the storehouse, which is the church that feeds you. It is a devious mixing of Scriptures that have little to do with each other yet are tied together for the purpose of forcing you to give them your money. As we saw with tithing, first fruits were established as part of the Mosaic Law for the governance of the theocracy of Israel. While the Leviticus verses established the feast of first fruits, these verses get into the details of carrying it out. We still do not see anything monetary. Nothing about honoring the Lord with your increase. It also has little to do with tithing. The system of tithing was entirely different. Tithing had to do with the Levitical priest system, and first fruits was a feast of remembrance. The tithing teacher, however, tries to conflate the two. He tries to convince you that the principle of first fruits demands that you obey the tithing system. It is at best inaccurate and at worst a willful deliberate attempt to steal your money.

Deuteronomy 18:1-5 Updated American Standard Version (UASV)

18 "The Levitical priests, all the tribe of Levi, shall have no portion or inheritance with Israel. They shall eat Jehovah's food offerings as his[135] inheritance. ² They shall have no inheritance among their brothers; Jehovah is their inheritance, as he promised them.

³ And this shall be the priests' due from the people, from those offering a sacrifice, whether an ox or a sheep: they shall give to the priest the shoulder and the two cheeks and the stomach. ⁴ The firstfruits of your grain, of your wine and of your oil, and the first fleece of your sheep, you shall give him. ⁵ For Jehovah your God has chosen him out of all your tribes to stand and minister in the name of Jehovah, him and his sons forever.

I list Deuteronomy 18 after the verses from chapter 26 because 26 deals with the explanation of first fruits and 18 uses the term first fruits. In simple terms, first fruits mean exactly that, the first of what you produce. These verses from chapter 18 are dealing with the Levitical priest system; not the feast of first fruits. Why then is the term used? Because the tithing system was a system of taking the first 10% of what was produced for the Levites. No one is disputing that. The cleverness of the first fruit equals tithing argument is that it is backwards. A tithe within the Levitical priest system is the first fruits, 10%, of what was produced. What the tithing teachers try to do is the inverse. They pretend that because there was a

---

[135] I.e. *their inheritance*

feast of first fruits, it established a biblical principle that reinforces the Levitical tithing system. Once again deft sleight of hand to dupe the sheep. I want to review one other Old Testament Scripture:

Proverbs 3:9-10 Updated American Standard Version (UASV)

⁹ Honor Jehovah with your wealth
and with the firstfruits of all your produce;
¹⁰ then your barns will be filled with plenty,
and your vats will be bursting with wine.

Let me start by saying that Proverbs are not meant to be wielded like doctrinal and universal truths. They are guidelines or guardrails if you will. It is still the Word of God, but they should be used in a complimentary fashion, not as a standalone definition of universal principles. Anything that God intended as a universal principle will be supported throughout Scripture like we saw earlier with sowing and reaping. Yes, there is a proverb that speaks to sowing and reaping, but there are at least two other very specific scriptural instances that reinforce that principle. While we are on the subject, this proverb only reinforces the principle of sowing and reaping. Remember, no one is advocating to not give into the work of the kingdom. When we find a gospel-centric church that does not compromise we will not find a more suitable place to "sow." Wait a minute preacher! I thought you said the seed sowing was heresy! The way the charlatans present it is heresy because the harvest is always temporal gain for you instead of eternal gain for the glory of God. There is no disputing there is a harvest coming:

Matthew 9:37-38 Updated American Standard Version (UASV)

³⁷ Then he said to his disciples, "The harvest is plentiful, but the workers are few. ³⁸ Therefore, beg the Master of the harvest to send out workers into his harvest."

We are the laborers, but the harvest is Gods. It belongs to Him. It does not consist of wealth transfers, uncommon favor seeds, or any other manmade nonsense. The harvest is a harvest of souls into the kingdom. I want to show you now the typical false tithing teachers' first fruit scam. This is taken from Paula White's website:

To be in alignment with what God has for us, we must start the year off as instructed- by obeying God's Holy Principle! God's Word clearly instructs us..."When you come into the land which I give you and reap its harvest, then you shall bring a sheaf of the first fruits of your harvest to the priest," Leviticus 23:10. It is to be set apart as holy unto God! 2014 is a powerful year of "Double Portion." The number "7" means "Perfection." The number "14" means "Double Perfection"...a Double Portion! Your First Fruits this year is the "Activation" of the double portion! Isaiah 61:7, "Instead of your shame you will receive a double portion, and instead of disgrace you will rejoice in your inheritance. And so you will inherit a double portion in your land, and everlasting joy will be yours."

We touched earlier on the propensity of these false teachers to dabble in numerology to sell their heresies. Numerology is simply put witchcraft and it is demonic. Seven is the number of perfection so 14 must mean double perfection? What is that? It doesn't even make any sense logically! Can perfection be doubled? Not according to the English language. Based on this logic I can't wait for the year 2049 so I can have seven times the perfection! Stop the nonsense! It doesn't even sound spiritual. It sounds moronic. To then take the ridiculous "double perfection" and translate it into double portion and somehow apply Isaiah 61 to us today is Scriptural abuse. What is more revealing however is her assertion at the start. We must start the year off as instructed - by obeying God's Holy Principle? Really? Maybe she should have studied her Jewish feasts. The verse she quotes we already saw was from the establishment of the feast of first fruits. If she studied, maybe she would have realized that first fruits is the third feast of the year, not the first. Maybe then she could have realized that there is no holy principle of first fruits. Do you see the scam already though? Takes the focus off of herself and onto God, pretending He is asking for your money. That He has ordained it as a principle in His Word. She even throws in a couple of Scriptures figuring you will never do the work of a Berean and actually check them. Seriously, who is going to read Isaiah and Leviticus? Especially when there is a double portion hanging in the balance! Double portion of what? Let us continue with the sales pitch:

You must "hear" this powerful revelation given for you that will transform you in ways you could never imagine in 2014! You have a "promise to come" from the Lord for the New Year, one that includes a release of blessing for your well being, your spirit, your soul, your body, your marriage, your relationships, your finances... EVERYTHING! Because it is about putting First Things First! Putting God First!

You have a promise to come for this year! Released blessings in your spirit, soul, body, marriage, relationships, finances and EVERYTHING! Do we even realize how utterly stupid this is? Does anyone think God operates like this? That everyone who buys her series will have blessings released into every area of their life? So, if 2000 people bought it, all 2000 would receive blessings in everything they do and have in their lives? No one in the valley? No sickness? No problems? No struggles? Just for the people who were lucky enough to come across this message from one lady in Florida. How completely ludicrous. White continues:

First Fruits in Hebrew is "bikkurim" and literally means "promise to come." And there is ONE who never breaks His promise – God! That is why the truth behind this "promise to come" in God's Word is so powerful. Though long overlooked by many, this divine establishment of God's order of things is actually the root that governs the rest. When you KEEP FIRST THINGS FIRST through faith and obedience, you turn God's promise into provision... ABUNDANT PROVISION!

Now she moves in for the kill. Having already established a fake principle, she now claims everything in our life works off of this fake principle. That God, not her, has promised this already and that our faith in obedience activates God to turn that promise into provision. Now that's a lot of religious-speak so let me translate it into English for you. If you give her money she promises that God will provide it back unto you. That is what she means by "keeping first things first." It harkens back to the faulty premise of first fruits. Back to the newsletter:

Because He wants to see you succeed, He has put a system into place based on the principle of "First Fruits." The Bible references first fruits or first things or devoted things no less than 32 times.

"Honor the Lord with your wealth, with the first fruits of all your increase" (Proverbs 3:9).

"When you come into the land which I gave you, and reap its harvest, then you shall bring a sheaf of the first fruits of your harvest to the priest" (Leviticus 23:9-10)

God claims the first fruits of anything! It rightfully belongs to Him in His divine order. When we apply the Principle of First Fruits – First Things First – in our lives, we begin to see that all firsts should be given to the Lord: the first part of the day, the first day of the week (Sabbath), the first month of the year, and the first of our harvest – be it the wages for the first hour, the first day, the first week, or the month.

Yes Paula, and the vast majority of those 32 times it has to do with the Levitical priest system or the feast God set up. It has nothing to do with a "principle" where people today have to send you money in order to have God's provision, a double perfection portion, or any other nonsense you want to make up to fleece God's flock. Once again though, White provides Scriptures counting on the majority to never check. We covered both of these already. Leviticus was where the feast was established, and Proverbs reinforces the sowing and reaping principle, not a tithe-like system. Even if somehow you could convince someone that this really was a principle, it still remains related to Israel and the management of a theocracy that has been defunct for over two millennia. Hebrews 7 still eradicates it.

2Corinthians 9 still represents giving as God intends for the New Covenant. Paula's newsletter continues:

> You can put God first in every area of your life by:
> - PRAYING. Give God your first thoughts in the morning. Talk with Him before you do anything else EVERY day. Pray without ceasing for your family, for financial recovery and blessings, for healing... for your needs. God will honor your faithfulness.
> - PLANNING. Where do you want to be 365 days from today? Getting from here to there requires a prayerful plan. Seek God's clear directive for your life, then write it down. Keep it in the front of you on a daily basis. Let it get into your spirit. See it! Believe it! Live it!
> - MAKING AN OFFERING. When you give your first fruits offering, you are planting a seed for the remainder of the year. Everything you have is a gift from God... you have an option to keep it or to sow it for an even greater harvest. There is a greater portion that awaits you in honor of your first fruits offering!

And at last we come to it. Blatant seed-sower theology. Sure she was slick enough to couch it by talking about prayer and planning first but the "offering" is the entire point of this newsletter. A greater portion awaits you if you would just be willing to sow a first fruits offering into Paula White's pocketbook...I mean ministry. Her net worth is only around five million dollars now. She needs more first fruits. White concludes:

> When you offer God your first fruits and bring Him the fullness of the first, you establish the foundation that the "whole thing" - your entire life – will be holy and blessed!
>
> I challenge you to put FIRST THINGS FIRST and HONOR GOD! Start activating the Word by offering God your FIRST FRUITS as a seed for your harvest in 2014. As you sacrifice your offering to Him, you set a precedent of what will come. You release a great promise of provision as a result of your obedience. Many people give a week's salary, others a day's, but everyone must give their very best offering!

How evil is this? To make up a principle by piecing together verses that are not related and now to claim that if you just send her money your entire life will be holy and blessed? To further claim that giving her money will activate the Word? To then have the audacity to essentially ask people for a week's worth of their wages? Absolutely shameless are the wolves fleecing the flock of Almighty God.

The lie of first fruits is possibly the most dangerous because it is conceptually mentioned a lot in the Old Testament as a system Israel had to follow. The vast majority of those references however dealt with two very specific things that have nothing to do with sowing seeds into the pockets of millionaire preachers today. The first is dealing with a specific feast that God ordained for Israel to remember His deliverance of them from slavery in Egypt. The second is in direct relation to the tithe system for the Levitical priests. Neither has anything to do with setting up a principle to be followed by believers today. If that was God's intent, he would have made it abundantly clear. Allow me to illustrate:

Galatians 6:7-8 Updated American Standard Version (UASV)

7 Do not be deceived: God is not to be mocked, for whatever a person sows, this he will also reap. 8 For the one who sows to his own flesh will from the flesh reap corruption, but the one who sows to the Spirit will from the Spirit reap eternal life.

Leviticus 23:9-10 Updated American Standard Version (UASV)

9 And Jehovah spoke to Moses, saying, 10 "Speak to the sons of Israel and say to them, 'When you come into the land that I give you and reap its harvest, you shall bring the sheaf of the firstfruits of your harvest to the priest.

The Galatians verses spell out in no uncertain terms what the principle is. Sow to the spirit and reap eternal life. Sow to the flesh and reap corruption. Nothing has to be massaged. Nothing has to be assumed. Nothing has to be interpreted. Additionally, it is supported by two other Scriptures that are just as bedrock solid:

2 Corinthians 9:6 Updated American Standard Version (UASV)

6 Now as to this, he who sows sparingly will also reap sparingly, and he who sows bountifully will also reap bountifully.

Proverbs 11:24 Updated American Standard Version (UASV)

24 One man scatters[136] freely, yet grows all the richer;
  another withholds what he should give, and only suffers want.

Are there any leaps in logic needed to understand these verses? No. Yet look at the verses from Leviticus. When you consider the context, it is clear these verses are dealing with the feast of first fruits. Then the tithing teacher wants you to look at verses that have to do with a Levitical priest system set up for Israel thousands of years ago. Then he scours the bible to find any use of the word "tithe" and finds them one time each in the life of Abram and Jacob, neither of which had anything to do with giving, blessings from God, or the eventual law. Then he wants you to look at

---

[136] The Hebrew verb (*pā·zǎr*) means to scatter: to spread, to distribute, to give to another implying generosity, a figurative expression of sowing seed

where Jesus told the Pharisees they ought to tithe but don't want you to realize that tithing is considered a negative in that story; a source of pride. The tithing teacher then wants you to look at Hebrews 7, which declares Christ as our High Priest and because in recounting the Abram story the word tithe is used again. It doesn't mean anything other than to set the background for why Jesus is the new High Priest in a letter to Messianic Jews. Somehow then the tithing teacher wants you to pretend they all are related, and God is secretly implementing a principle based on this conglomeration of verses that requires you to hand over 10% of your income to them. That is beyond a leap beloved; it is a chasm. The first fruits lie, while more devious and clever, is equally as false when held up to the plumb line of the Word of God.

CHAPTER ELEVEN The Cursed Money Lie

"The only reason I'm asking you to do this (tithe) is for your own good....I'm tired of hearing about families that are losing jobs and losing income and losing family and losing kids and losing marriages, because the devourer is devouring them. And he tells us very simply 'if you bring the tithe to the storehouse I (God) will rebuke the devourer for your sake.' It's a pretty good deal for 10%." - Robert Morris

"Don't give the first portion [of your income] to the mortgage company because the mortgage company does not have the power to bless your finances. Only God does. Don't give the first portion to the electric company, the electric company cannot bless your finances, only God can. Would you rather live with 100% of your income and all of it cursed, or 90% of your income and all of it blessed. That's what the Bible says." - Robert Morris

I have to be honest - I just do not understand how some of the false preachers live with themselves. I do not understand how they operate within the things of God without the fear of God. I find myself making excuses; thinking that maybe they are sincere but sincerely wrong. While I am sure that is the case for many I continue to think that many more know exactly what they are doing. Surely, they must. Enter this chapter's heretic, Robert Morris. Morris is the Pastor at Gateway Church in Dallas Texas, which averages about 20,000 attendees per week. He is a megachurch pastor to say the least. What he is probably best known for however is being the poster child for abusing the tithing message that churches are propped up by today. Morris is so good at this fleecing shtick that he is frequently asked by other wolves to preach tithing to their sheep. He has preached at Rick Warren's Saddleback Church and the second quote above was taken from a sermon at Life Church. He is so popular that his cursed money theology is endorsed by the new head of the Southern Baptist Convention, Ronnie Floyd.

Take a good long look at these quotes from Morris. Beloved this is most certainly NOT what the Bible says. I have seen and heard of the most abusive tactics used by preachers in the name of tithing. I have heard preachers advocate people give them their last $50 so God "has something to work with." Now we have this latest garbage from Morris. Actually guilting people into ignoring their responsibilities of homeownership or keeping their utilities turned on so they can send him money. The height of disgusting. If you are in a church that spreads nonsense like this, you must understand it is nothing more than bondage. It is not from God at all and His Word proves so:

1 Timothy 5:8 Updated American Standard Version (UASV)

8 But if anyone does not provide for his own,[137] and especially for those of his household, he has denied the faith and is worse than an unbeliever.

Yet to hear Morris and others preach they say do not pay your bills. They say to tithe first. Not satisfied with merely ripping verses violently out of context they take it a step further and mangle the Scriptures. To preach this cursing lie Morris relies of course on Malachi Chapter Three:

Malachi 3:8-12 Updated American Standard Version (UASV)

8 Will a human dare to rob God? Yet you are robbing me! And you say, 'How have we robbed you?' In the tenth parts [138] and the offerings 9 You are cursed with a curse, for you are robbing me, the whole nation of you. 10 Bring all the tenth parts[139] into the storehouse, that there may be food in my house. And thereby put me to the test, says Jehovah of armies,[140] if I will not open the windows of heaven for you and pour down for you a blessing until there is nothing lacking. 11 I will rebuke the devourer for you, so that it will not destroy the fruits of your soil, and your vine in the field will not fail to bear, says Jehovah of armies. 12 Then all nations will call you blessed, for you will be a land of delight, says Jehovah of armies.

I am sure we remember these verses from the chapter dealing with Malachi, but it is important to see how Morris lifts out the portions he then

---

[137] I.e., *relatives*
[138] I.e. *tithes*
[139] I.e. *the full tithe*. The Mosaic Law was eliminated by Jesus' death, so monetary tithing is no longer a requirement. However, tithing has a figurative meaning. (Eph. 2:15) It does not symbolize the giving of our all. While the tenth part was brought every year, Christians now bring their all to the Father only once, when they dedicate themselves to him and symbolize their dedication by being water in water. It is whatever our situations allow, and our heart motivates us to use. The offerings we bring to the Father can be time, energy, and resources used in our carrying out the will of the Father, which would include attending Christian meetings, visiting sick ones and the elderly believers, and offering whatever financial support our heart moves us to give to God.
[140] **Jehovah of armies:** (Heb. *jhvh tsaba*) literally means an army of soldiers, or military forces (Gen. 21:22; Deut. 20:9). It can also be used figuratively, "the sun and the moon and the stars, all the armies of heaven." (Deut. 4:19) In the plural form, it is also used of the Israelites forces as well. (Ex. 6:26; 7:4; Num. 33:1; Psa. 44:9) However, the "armies" in the expression "Jehovah of armies" is a reference to the angelic forces primarily, if not exclusively.

wields against the sheep. The tithe teacher will say, "But look! The verses clearly say you are cursed for robbing God of His tithes and offerings!" Let us reflect back to earlier in the book. Who is the Book of Malachi addressed to? That's right the priests. As if to avoid any confusion, God already has mentioned this curse earlier in Malachi:

Malachi 2:1-2 Updated American Standard Version (UASV)

2 "And now, O priests, this command is for you. ² If you will not listen, if you will not take it to heart to give honor to my name, says Jehovah of armies, then I will send the curse upon you and I will curse your blessings. Yes, I have already cursed them, because you do not lay it to heart.

And now PRIESTS. Not the people. This is one of the biggest cons in the church every week. Quoting Malachi to produce tithing. What is this curse that God is warning the priests of? Is it something the Israelites would recognize? Absolutely. It is a reminder of the end of the Torah:

Deuteronomy 27:26 Updated American Standard Version (UASV)

²⁶ 'Cursed be anyone who does not confirm the words of this law by doing them.' And all the people shall say, 'Amen.'

The curse spoken of in Malachi is the curse of the law. Those that could not keep the law were subject to many curses. There are 53 verses of curses in Deuteronomy 28 alone! This message was not lost on the Israelites of this time. They were the formerly exiled remnant that spent 70 years in captivity in Babylon. They saw God deliver the curses of Deuteronomy 28 upon them. The larger point for us as believers in Jesus Christ is our relationship to the law. The Apostle Paul explains:

Galatians 3:10-14 Updated American Standard Version (UASV)

¹⁰ For as many as are of the works of the law are under a curse, for it is written, "Cursed is everyone who does not abide by all the things that are written in the book of the law to do them."[141] ¹¹ Now that no one is justified by the law before God is evident; for, "The righteous man shall live by faith." ¹² But the law is not of faith, rather "The one who does them shall live by them." ¹³ Christ redeemed us from the curse of the law by becoming a curse for us, because it is written, "Cursed is everyone who hangs on a tree,"[142] ¹⁴ in order that in Christ Jesus the blessing of Abraham

---

[141] Quote from Deut. 27:26
[142] Quote from Deut. 21:23

might come to the Gentiles, so that we would receive the promise of the Spirit through faith.

What part of this do the tithing teachers not understand? By preaching tithing they are in fact yoking believers back to the law which Christ died to fulfill. The heresy from Morris and company about curses though is even more of an affront to Jesus because they are trying to lay the exact curse Christ set us free from back upon us. How dare they. Jesus Himself mentioned tithing three times in the Gospel accounts. Here they are:

Matthew 23:23-24 Updated American Standard Version (UASV)

[23] "Woe to you, scribes and Pharisees, hypocrites! because you give the tenth of the mint and the dill and the cumin, but you have disregarded the weightier matters of the Law, namely, justice and mercy and faithfulness. These things it was necessary to do, yet not to disregard the other things. [24] Blind guides, who strain out a gnat and swallow a camel!

Luke 11:42 Updated American Standard Version (UASV)

"But woe to you Pharisees! For you tithe mint and rue and every herb, and neglect justice and the love of God. These you ought to have done, without neglecting the others.

Luke 18:9-14 Updated American Standard Version (UASV)

[9] He also told this parable to some who trusted in themselves that they were righteous, and treated others with contempt: [10] "Two men went up into the temple to pray, one a Pharisee and the other a tax collector. [11] The Pharisee stood and prayed these things to himself: 'God, I thank you that I am not like other men, extortioners, unjust, adulterers, or even like this tax collector. [12] I fast twice a week; I give a tenth of all that I get.' [13] But the tax collector, standing at a distance, was not willing even to raise his eyes to heaven but kept beating his breast, saying, 'God, be merciful to me, a sinner!' [14] I tell you, this man went to his house justified rather than the other; for everyone who exalts himself will be humbled, but he who humbles himself will be exalted."

I ask you, is tithing being lifted up in any of these verses? I see plenty of times people use the fact that Jesus never addressed something as an excuse to sin, but you cannot say He never addressed tithing. He addressed it twice (the first two sets of verses are the same account in two different Gospels). In these first two sets of Scriptures, Jesus actually pronounces a woe upon the tithers! What is a woe? It is a curse! If I created doctrine like Robert Morris, I would teach that Jesus cursed tithers and so should we! Obviously, that was not what Jesus was saying. He was, however, pointing out that the Pharisees focused on the lesser important matters, such as tithing. They ignored the weightier matters such as mercy, justice and faithfulness. That does not help the pro tithing preachers very much either!

Let us look at the last set of verses here though. This is Jesus telling the Parable of the Pharisee and the Tax Collector. Jesus always used striking examples that would resonate in the minds of His listeners. He chose a Samaritan in the Parable of the Good Samaritan to be the hero because He knew about the prejudice of the Jewish people towards the Samaritans. In this parable, He chose another reviled person to be the hero, a tax collector. In these days, the Jews who were tax collectors were despised because they worked for Rome and often cheated their own people to make extra profit. They were like the tithing preachers of today in that regard. In this parable, however, we see the tax collector was the one with true humility before God. The Pharisee, who regarded himself as super-spiritual was the one who was not justified. What was one of the things Jesus said He bragged about? Tithing! Realize this is a fictitious story Jesus made up to drive home a point about pride and humility before God. Isn't it a bit odd that He would make a point of showing tithing as a source of pride if He intended it to carry on as a universal principle? Yet another death blow to the tithing argument.

Is God going to curse you for not tithing? Of course not. In fact, we end up cursed if we do tithe because we are taking back the yoke of bondage according to the Apostle Paul in Galatians:

Galatians 5:1-6 Updated American Standard Version (UASV)

5 For freedom Christ has set us free; stand firm therefore, and do not submit again to a yoke of slavery.

2 Behold I, Paul, say to you that if you receive circumcision, Christ will be of no benefit to you. 3 And I testify again to every man who receives circumcision, that he is under obligation to keep the whole law. 4 You are severed from Christ, you who would be[143] justified by the law; you have fallen away from grace. 5 For we through the Spirit, by faith, are waiting for the hope of righteousness. 6 For in Christ Jesus neither circumcision nor uncircumcision means anything, but faith working through love.

This is very important beloved. The Galatians at this time were being infiltrated by the Judaizers. These were Jewish Christians who wanted to mix some of the law in with the grace that set them free. This is what Paul is speaking to here. He is saying to the Galatian believers to stand firm in the freedom of Christ and do not submit again to the yoke of slavery. What

---

[143] Or *are seeking* or *are attempting*

is slavery? The law! If they accept circumcision, a requirement of the law, then they are obligated to keep the whole law. They are severed from Christ. They have fallen away from grace. Christ is of no advantage to them. Now is the issue circumcision? No beloved; it is the law. It can be any part of the law because just like breaking one meant you broke them all, living by one means you must try to live by them all! That includes tithing. Let us see what this section of Scripture would have looked like if the Judaizers were trying to reinforce tithing instead of circumcision:

For freedom Christ has set us free; stand firm therefore, and do not submit again to a yoke of slavery. Look: I, Paul, say to you that if you accept tithing, Christ will be of no advantage to you. I testify again to every man who accepts tithing that he is obligated to keep the whole law. You are severed from Christ, you who would be justified by the law; you have fallen away from grace. For through the Spirit, by faith, we ourselves eagerly wait for the hope of righteousness. For in Christ Jesus neither tithing nor not tithing counts for anything, but only faith working through love.

Before anyone gets in a tizzy; I am not changing the Word of God. I am merely making a visual point. Those who preach tithing curses do not realize the frightening truth may be that preaching tithing alone is a curse. Making people submit again to the yoke of the slavery of the law. By doing so, they now are open for the rest of the law. Christ is rendered of no advantage anymore. Sobering thoughts indeed.

CHAPTER TWELVE The More Absurd Lies

I know the title of this chapter may make some wonder what could be more absurd than some of what we have already reviewed but there have been even crazier attempts to fleece the flock. Tithing teachers get so desperate sometimes they overreach in their attempt to swindle the people of God. This chapter will delve into some of the more bizarre lies. The first example is the story of Ananias and Sapphira. I actually heard a tithing teacher one time try and use this story to defend the tithing system. He was browbeating his sheep when he said, "If you do not think God takes this serious, perhaps you should ask Ananias and Sapphira! You can't because God struck them dead for holding back what belonged to God!" I kid you not. Here are the Scriptures:

Acts 5:1-11 Updated American Standard Version (UASV)

5 But a man named Ananias, with his wife Sapphira, sold a piece of property, 2 and he held back some of the price for himself, with his wife's knowledge, and he brought just a part of it and deposited it at the feet of the apostles. 3 But Peter said, "Ananias, why has Satan filled your heart to lie to the Holy Spirit and to keep back for yourself part of the proceeds of the land? 4 While it remained unsold, did it not remain your own? And after it was sold, was it not at your disposal? Why is it that you have contrived this deed in your heart? You have not lied to man but to God." 5 When Ananias heard these words, he fell down and breathed his last; and great fear came upon all who heard of it. 6 The young men rose and wrapped him up and carried him out and buried him.

7 After an interval of about three hours his wife came in, not knowing what had happened. 8 And Peter said to her, "Tell me whether you[144] sold the land for so much." And she said, "Yes, for so much." 9 But Peter said to her, "How is it that you have agreed together to test the Spirit of the Lord? Look, the feet of those who have buried your husband are at the door, and they will carry you out." 10 And immediately she fell down at his feet and breathed her last. When the young men came in they found her dead, and they carried her out and buried her beside her

---

[144] The Greek for *you* is plural

husband. [11] And great fear came upon the whole congregation[145] and upon all who heard of these things.

So, the question before us is what is this story about? What is the context? For that we have to go back into chapter four and discover that in the early church, everyone was sharing what they had so no one was in need. Right before this story we saw Barnabas had sold a field and laid the money at the feet of the Apostles. Then for contrast, we have the story of this married couple, Ananias and Sapphira. What do we know based on the biblical text?

* The couple sold a piece of property and knowingly held back some of the money for themselves.

* This was a lie to the Holy Spirit because they tried to pretend they were giving everything, as Barnabas had done.

* They did not have to give anything. They also could have kept whatever they wanted. The issue was the lying and pretending they gave all the proceeds.

* God struck them both dead for this sin.

So, what in the world does this have to do with tithing? For that matter what does it even have to do with money? The answer is nothing. It has everything to do with hypocrisy. God did not strike them dead because they held back what belonged to God. The text makes it clear that all of the money was theirs to do with as they pleased. It was the trying to look better than they were. I refer to Ananias and Sapphira as the first religious spirit in the church. Trying to look more pious than they really were. Here are some comments from Kenneth O. Gangel in *Acts*, vol. 5, Holman New Testament Commentary:

Honor and Dishonor in the Church

MAIN IDEA: *God will allow nothing to stand in the way of the proclamation of his gospel and the expansion of his church.*

A. Rebellion in the Church (vv. 1–4)

---

[145] **Congregation:** (Heb. *qahal*; Gr. *ekklesia*) A congregation of Christians. A group of Christians, who gather for a Christian meeting, implying an interacting membership. In the Hebrew Scriptures, it usually refers to the nation of Israel, i.e., "the assembly of Israel" or "the congregation of Israel." In the Greek New Testament, it refers to congregations of Christians, as well as the Christian congregation as a whole. – Num. 20:8; Deut. 4:10; 1 Ki 8:22; Ac 9:31; Rom. 16:5; 1 Cor. 14:4.

> **SUPPORTING IDEA:** *God knows when you are lying to him and will not let you stand in the way of the proclamation of his gospel.*
>
> **5:1–2.** Like Paul, Luke is ever the master of contrast. Immediately following the brief testimony of Barnabas, he tells us about two other Christians who sold property so they could participate in the church's communal care program. The name Ananias means "God is gracious," and Sapphira means "beautiful." This was a joint effort even if the cultural patterns of the time put Ananias first. Luke tells us **he kept back part of the money**, using the verb *nospizo* which means "to put aside for oneself." Already this narrative reminds us of Achan in Joshua 7:1–26.
>
> This couple wanted acclaim without sacrifice and comfort without commitment. They caused the first demonstration of defeat within the ranks since the betrayal of Judas and denial by Peter. The outward act seemed so appropriate. Notice the identical wording in 4:37 and 5:2: **Put it at the apostles' feet**. What appeared to be public generosity was actually family conspiracy, but God was looking.
>
> **5:3–4.** Apparently, the Holy Spirit revealed this deception to Peter. The Spirit had created unity in the church and was now offended at its rupture. We are amazed to discover that Satan can fill the heart of a Christian, especially since Luke uses a verb for *fill* which also appears in Ephesians 5:18.
>
> Peter faced up to the responsibility much in the way he did in chapter 1 when explaining the Judas suicide. We see immediately that the sin lay not in failing to give all the money, but rather in pretending to do so. The basic issue here was lying, not only to the church but to the Spirit. Above all, the church had to maintain integrity in its alien surroundings, and this behavior could quickly erode the shields of that credibility. Integrity describes those standards of moral and intellectual honesty on which we base our conduct and from which we cannot swerve without cheapening ourselves.
>
> This passage also offers an important New Testament text on the deity of the Holy Spirit. Peter tells Ananias that he lied to the Holy Spirit and follows by saying, **You have not lied to men but to God**. Notice the emphasis on the voluntary nature of participation in communal property. Some see Communism at the end of chapter 4, but Peter makes it clear that Ananias was under no obligation to participate. Once he did,

however, he betrayed the unity and community of the congregation. Tom Constable writes,

> Lying to the Holy Spirit is a sin that Christians commit frequently today. When Christians act hypocritically by pretending a devotion that is not there or a surrender of life that they have not really made, they lie to the Holy Spirit. If God worked today as he did in the early Jerusalem church, undertakers would have much work (Constable, 39).

B. Reaction to the Crime (vv. 5–11)

SUPPORTING IDEA: *Sickness and death do not always result from sin, but God reserves the right to deal with sin in his church, even to the strongest possible penalty.*

5:5–6. We are stunned to read the results of Ananias' lie—God killed him. The word for died is *ekpsycho*, "to breathe one's last," used of General Sisera in the Septuagint of Judges 4:21 (cf. Acts 5:10; 12:23). We will deal with this judgment at greater length in "Deeper Discoveries." Here we should not obscure the clarity of the text. We can explain what happened. We must still remember God is the ultimate cause. One psychological explanation of what happened suggests that Ananias died from the shock of discovery. As one commentator puts it, "The fear of exposure was so drastic, their nervous systems could not take it" (Ogilvie, 120). To be sure, death from seemingly natural causes could have its origin in a supernatural act (as in the case of Herod at the end of Acts 12), but it is no less God ordained. Here we have the ultimate discipline in the church. God can remove a spiritual cancer by surgery and may very well choose to do so on some occasions (1 Cor. 11:30–32).

In this case the death resulted from sin, but the Bible reminds us that immediate death does not always occur. In the early verses of John 9, the disciples concluded that the blind man must be suffering because of his sin or that of his parents. Jesus reminds them that neither is the case, "But this happened so that the work of God might be displayed in his life" (John 9:3). God sees what happens in our hearts; and when hidden sin threatens to thwart the church's ministry, he may choose to deal with it severely.

5:7–10. The young attendants had buried Ananias and returned in three hours, quite possibly a record for first-century Jewish funerals. Amazingly, Sapphira came in with the same story, and it was deja vu all over again. Sapphira's narrative offers nothing new. In neither case did

> Peter pronounce a curse of any kind. Peter explained the sin, but God took care of the judgment.
>
> **5:11.** The death of Ananias and Sapphira brought two results: fear in the church and fear in the city. This is the first appearance in Acts of the Greek word for church *(ekklesia)*. Perhaps Peter remembered this incident when he wrote: "It is time for judgment to begin with the family of God" (1 Pet. 4:17). Fear in the city centered on the power of God and perhaps the ugliness of sin.
>
> As tempted as we might be to push this story into some dark corner of early church history, that would be a tragic mistake. It deals with money, greed, and deceit—all very popular problems in today's church. Deceit, disunity, and duplicity always undermine the Holy Spirit's work and always erode the effectiveness of the Christian community.[146]

To try and say this story has anything to do with tithing is beyond unreasonable. It is bizarre. The next example we have is the Garden of Eden. Yes, you heard me right. There are some tithing crazies who insist that tithing goes way back to the first story of man in the Bible. What a coup it would be if it were true, but of course it is not even close to truth. Here is basic argument taken from the writings of the late Dr. Norman Wells, former pastor at Cincinnati's Central Baptist Church:

The principle of tithing began in the Garden of Eden. The tithe is that part of our possessions that God sets apart for Himself. "... all the tithe ... is the Lord's ..." Lev. 27:30. God demonstrated this principle in the Garden of Eden. God gave Adam and Eve the free use of the garden for their own sustenance and pleasure, however, He reserved a portion of the garden and forbade them to partake. By refraining from partaking of God's reserved part of the garden, Adam and Eve demonstrated their obedience to God and acknowledged Him as their God. This is the principle of tithing! Adam and Eve, like so many since, were not satisfied with the portion God had given them and they partook of God's reserved part. It seems a great number have inherited this characteristic of not being satisfied with nine-tenths but desire God's reserved one-tenth. It brought judgment to the violators in the garden—it brings judgment today.

---

[146] Kenneth O. Gangel, *Acts*, vol. 5, Holman New Testament Commentary (Nashville, TN: Broadman & Holman Publishers, 1998), 74–76.

Let us start with the obvious. Tithing was a system set up for the management of the nation of Israel and consisted of setting aside the first tenth of your agricultural increase. It is not about God withholding something. The parallel is silly. Secondly, according to this logic there must have been only ten trees in the Garden of Eden. That is a mighty small garden. What does Scripture say:

Genesis 2:10-14 Updated American Standard Version (UASV)

¹⁰ Now a river flowed out[147] of Eden to water the garden; and from there it divided and became four rivers.[148] ¹¹ The name of the first is Pishon; it flows around the whole land of Havilah, where there is gold. ¹² And the gold of that land is good; bdellium and onyx stone are there. ¹³ The name of the second river is Gihon; it flows around the whole land of Cush. ¹⁴ The name of the third river is Tigris; it flows east of Assyria.[149] And the fourth river is the Euphrates.

A garden with ten trees that needs a river to water it? That river then became four rivers? That doesn't sound right. No, I am pretty sure the garden was substantial. Ten percent of it would not be one tree. There is the notion that God reserved a portion of the garden. Dr. Wells and tithing teachers need to spin it this way to set it up as being a model for tithing. It completely misses the point. God did not reserve a portion of the garden. The one tree in question would kill His creation if they partook. That was the point:

Genesis 2:15-17 Updated American Standard Version (UASV)

¹⁵ And Jehovah God took the man and set him in the garden of Eden to cultivate it and to keep it. ¹⁶ And Jehovah God commanded the man, saying, "From every tree of the garden you may freely eat, ¹⁷ but from the tree of the knowledge of good and evil you shall not eat,[150] for in the day that you eat from it you shall surely die."[151]

So yes, technically by refusing to eat of the tree they were being obedient but there was a reason why. A very self-serving reason why. It certainly does not "establish the principle of tithing." If it were so established, why did God not bring it up again for 2500 years? Even if you want to pretend Abram and Jacob tithed; that is only two events in 2500 years! Nothing from Isaac, Joseph, Noah or any other person until it is

---

[147] Lit., *was going out*; Hebrew participle refers to a continuous stream
[148] Lit *became four heads*
[149] *Assyria* Heb., *Ashshur*
[150] Lit *eat from it*
[151] Lit *dying you* [singular] *shall die*. Heb *moth tamuth*; the first reference to death in the Scriptures

established in the Levitical code. It is preposterous to suggest that God established a universal principle of tithing in the Garden of Eden and then forgot about it for 2500 years. That aside, perhaps the most disturbing thing about this explanation is to propose that Adam and Eve were not satisfied with the portion God gave them and wanted to partake in the reserved part. Once again, that completely misses the mark:

Genesis 3:1-7 Updated American Standard Version (UASV)

3 Now the serpent was more crafty than any beast of the field which Jehovah God had made. And he said to the woman, "Did God actually say, 'You[152] shall not eat of any tree in the garden'?" **2** And the woman said to the serpent, "From the fruit of the trees of the garden we may eat, **3** but from the tree that is in the midst of the garden, God said, 'You shall not eat from it, nor shall you touch it, lest you die.'" **4** And the serpent said to the woman, "You shall not surely die. **5** For God knows that when you eat of it your eyes will be opened, and you will be like God, knowing good and evil." knowing good and evil.

6 So when the woman saw that the tree was good for food, and that it was a delight to the eyes, and that the tree was to be desirable to make one wise, and she took of its fruit and ate, then she also gave some to her husband when with her, and he ate. **7** Then the eyes of both of them were opened, and they knew that they were naked; and they sewed fig leaves together and made themselves loin coverings.

To the tithing teacher Adam and Eve were just not satisfied with what God had given them. They need that to be able to try and stretch this story into tithing because all of us cheap Christians are never satisfied and always want to take what belongs to God. This is beyond a stretch however when we examine the text. In order to simplify this story to only being about not being satisfied with their allotment you have ignore several things:

* The presence and lies of the enemy.

* The desire to be like God.

* The appeal of the fruit to her eyes.

* The appeal of the fruit for wisdom.

Beloved this is the great fall of man. The story that sets into cosmic motion the redemptive plan of God. The story that first prophesies the coming of our Lord and Savior Jesus Christ. The story that defines our sin

---

[152] In Hebrew *you* is plural in verses 1–5

nature. To take all of that and only see tithing is actually pretty sick. To then finish off your logic by saying judgment from God will still follow today for those who do not tithe is nothing short of abuse of the sheep of God. Adam and Eve and Ananias and Sapphira are theologically rich stories. One sets the foundation for the Old Testament and the other is one of the earliest foundational stories of the New Testament. They both contain the wrath of God and His abhorrence for sin. Adam and Eve lost their birthright, eternal life, and were forced out of the garden. Ananias and Sapphira were struck dead. All four succumbed to the wiles of the devil. All four believed his lies and paid horrible prices for it. All four of them and these two great stories have absolutely nothing to do with tithing. To come up with that and ignore all the power and doctrine contained in them shows beyond a doubt there is an agenda afoot that has nothing to do with God and everything to do with money.

Having said that we move on to the latest scheme in pushing tithing - the money back guarantee! Yes, that's right now you can try out what is supposed to be a God-honoring system, and if you do not like your rate of return, then you can get your money back! Megachurch pastors Ed Young and Robert Morris have offered this scam before; Morris requiring a year's worth of tithing! Megachurch pastor Perry Noble also has this as a staple of his church. Filled with the usual lineup of tithing clichés like, "You can't out give God" and "It all belongs to Him anyway", Noble goes a step further by saying at the end of the 90 days if you think God is a liar, then he will refund your money. I wonder how many actually request their money back if that is the caveat.

Here is the problem theologically for all of these scam artists. According to tithing teachers, the tithe is holy and belongs to God. They will all insist that you are not giving to them but to God. By telling you, they have the authority to give you this tithe back they are admitting that it does not belong to God but rather to them. The only other explanation is that they would then be robbing God. They would then be under the same curse they try to bestow upon you! The second big problem is the nature of the tithe they are selling. According to this logic, you tithe for a set period of time, and if you are not satisfied, you can get your money back. Satisfied with what? With God of course and His blessings. By default, they admit to selling the blessings of God. Taking it the next logical step, we find that they must believe that faithful tithing leads to permanent blessings. Never a time in the valley. Never a time of refinement or testing. No, it is all about the blessing machine that is their God, which apparently is coin operated.

Literally, as I am writing this book, I see new schemes emerging to defend tithing I had not previously heard of before. One such lie is that the law simply codified the established practice of tithing set in place by God. That the law regulated the tithe established by Abram. Not to sound like a broken record but this is simply untrue throughout. This is the continued conflation of tithing as a system and the word tithe being used to denote a tenth. The key however to the lie is in the assertion that tithing was ever established as a practice prior to the law and it simply was not. In fact, there is a period of 500 years between Abram and the law being established. Only one time is there a mention of a tithe, and that was the already discussed pagan tradition with the King Melchizedek. That is it. Abram did not establish tithing. In fact, he himself only gave a tenth once. There are no scriptural indications that tithing under the law was established because of this onetime event. Not only that but there is a key difference between law tithing and the one time Abram gave a tenth. Abram only gave of the spoils of war. Not one dime was given out of his personal wealth. Law tithing required the first ten percent agriculturally of increase. The true irony is that the tithing teachers trip over their own lies. Both first fruits and Abram tithed are lies, but there is absolutely no way they both could be true. So which is it? Did God establish first fruits and if He did why did Abram not give out of his personal increase? You cannot have it both ways. Either way, both are still lies. Then recently there was another pro tithing article written by a megachurch pastor Tom Brown. The Word of Life Church pastor offered a new twist on the argument about Matthew 23:23:

Some argue that Jesus words are not applicable to us today, because Jesus was under the Law and spoke to those under the Law. Their theory goes something like this: Jesus was giving an instruction to the Jews, so His words are not binding to us. The problem with this interpretation is that these teachers are bringing Christ down to the level of a Jewish prophet or Teacher of the Law. Jesus is the Word of God made flesh, so this means every word that comes out of His mouth is eternal. He cannot say anything without it being "spiritual law" and everlasting.

Matthew 23:23 is when Jesus is delivering the seven woes to the Pharisees, which we spoke about in detail in Chapter Seven. Jesus did indeed tell the Pharisees that they ought to tithe, but there are several problems with this new rationale to defend tithing. First, the issue is not that the words of Jesus are not binding to us it is that He was not speaking to us. This author would have us forget context and simply turn every word of Jesus into a spiritual law? Seriously? Passing words in conversation? Lazarus come forth? Woman, what does this have to do with me? Seriously? Let's test Pastor Brown's logic:

John 2:16 Updated American Standard Version (UASV)

¹⁶ And he told those who sold the doves, "Take these things away! Do not make my Father's house a market house."[153]

So according to this "every word is a spiritual law" theology, it is now a spiritual law that you cannot sell anything in the house of God. That's odd because on the Word of Life Church website you are free to order several books written by Pastor Tom Brown! This is the silliness of his argument. It takes everything literally and ignores the point. The point Jesus was making when He cleared the temple had to do with the corruption of the Pharisees who were price gouging foreigners and the poor. That is the lesson; not that you cannot sell something in the church. Likewise, when Jesus tells the Pharisees they ought to tithe, that was not the point He was trying to make:

Matthew 23:23-24 Updated American Standard Version (UASV)

²³ "Woe to you, scribes and Pharisees, hypocrites! because you give the tenth of the mint and the dill and the cumin, but you have disregarded the weightier matters of the Law, namely, justice and mercy and faithfulness. These things it was necessary to do, yet not to disregard the other things. ²⁴ Blind guides, who strain out a gnat and swallow a camel!

Remember this entire section is a series of curses upon the Pharisees. It was an outline of everything they were doing wrong. Only a tithing teacher can look at that vast context and single out the one thing Jesus said they were doing right as the point. Not only that but technically Jesus is using the contrast of tithing against the more important things they overlooked. Tithing had become a great source of pride for the Pharisees, as it is today for many Christians. What was the important takeaway from these two verses though? Justice, mercy, and faithfulness.

So, is every Word spoken by Christ eternal? Sure. Every Word in the Bible is eternal. That means it lasts forever. That means it maintains its power forever and will not fade. That does not, however, mean that everything He ever spoke hints to some eternal principle that He never spelled out. The point here though is about hypocrisy! Do not think yourself righteous because you tithe when you neglect the more important things of God! How in the world can you convince yourself that this is an advertisement for tithing is beyond me? Only greed can come to that decision.

---

[153] Or "a house of merchants" or "house of merchandise"

CHAPTER THIRTEEN Debunking Common Arguments

As we all know, the pro-tithers and tithing teachers will band together to insist that I am a heretic who is trying to steal your blessings. While I can assure you I am not, I thought it would be wise to review some of the common arguments you might hear and what the truth is. Some of this may have already been touched on, but it is worthy of another look.

Common Argument Number One - You're Just Stingy and Cheap

That isn't very nice considering you do not even know me! Seriously, I follow the Bible and the Bible alone. Not dogma handed down from generations long ago. My sincere belief is that when you find a good church, that preaches the uncompromised Gospel of Jesus Christ, then that should become your number one source of giving. It has to really fit that bill though and the majority of churches today do not. You can find good churches on the narrow path that leads to life. Get off that broad path that leadeth to destruction. That said, I also believe God mapped out for us the New Testament model for the church in Acts chapter 2:

Acts 2:42-47 Updated American Standard Version (UASV)

⁴² And they continued devoting themselves to the teaching of the apostles and to fellowship, to the breaking of bread and to prayers.¹⁵⁴ ⁴³ And fear came on every soul, and many wonders and signs were being performed through the apostles. ⁴⁴ And all those who believed were together and had all things in common; ⁴⁵ and they began selling their property and possessions and distributing these things to all, as anyone had need. ⁴⁶ Day by day continuing with one mind in the temple, and breaking bread from house to house, they were taking their food together with gladness and sincerity of heart, ⁴⁷ praising God and having favor with all the people. And the Lord added to their number day by day those who were being saved.

In this model, we are to devote ourselves to three things:

* Doctrine

* Fellowship with believers (including communion)

---

¹⁵⁴ Lit *the prayers*

* Prayer (individually and corporately)

When we do church as God designed we can expect real signs and wonders through the preaching of the Word. We are to be together because we have all things in common. They took care of each other, including financially. There have been many times over the years that I have extended a hand to brothers and sisters in need and in my time of need have found the same to be true. That is borderline anathema to tithing teachers who say the whole tithe is theirs. The important thing in this model for pastors to consider however is the last line. The model of the church God outlines has the vertical growth of the sheep be the responsibility of those who preach and teach. Discipling and bringing people to maturity in Christ. The horizontal growth, however, meaning how many new sheep are added to the flock, is the responsibility of God. This flies in the face of the Warren purpose driven model that names the pastor as the vision casting CEO who has to come up with creative ways to expand his church, usually at the expense of the Gospel. It is this wrongheaded mindset that often pushes pastors to be more militant about tithing because their vision is not God's vision and it requires more and more money to maintain. When finances do not equal the vision, it is always the sheep that are fault and not the vision casting CEO pastor.

I bring this up because, under the true model for the church, we are to truly be our brother's keeper and take care of each other in need. I have tried to live up to this. My issue with tithing has nothing to do with money. I tithed faithfully for many years at my old church when they were bringing the true Gospel. I was still learning to do the work of a Berean and discernment, however. I know this much. If I knew then what I know now, I would have been giving far above 10%. That was how much I believed in the work the church was doing and in my pastor. This may come as a shock to tithing teachers, but it is not all about money for everyone.

<u>Common Argument Number Two - Tithing Works For Me</u>

I have spoken to faithful brothers and sister who insist that tithing works for them. They tithe faithfully and see blessings in their life. I do not doubt them. They are simply mistaken about what is working. If we remember from chapter one, the New Testament model of giving is found in 2Corinthians 9, and it is bound by the principle of sowing and reaping. When you give faithfully into the work of God, it does not surprise me that blessings will come your way. I would like to add here that if you are faithful in tithing, I assume you are relatively faithful in other areas. It is not just about money. God does protect His children. He is an awesome and all-powerful God.

That said, tithing cannot be working for you because tithing does not exist. It has not existed for over 2000 years. Jesus nailed it to the cross:

Colossians 2:13-15 Updated American Standard Version (UASV)

[13] And you, who were dead in your trespasses [155] and the uncircumcision of your flesh, God made alive together with him, having forgiven us all our trespasses, [14] having canceled out the certificate of debt consisting of decrees against us, which was hostile to us; and he has taken it out of the way, having nailed it to the cross.[156] [15] having disarmed the rulers and authorities, he made a public display of them openly, triumphing over them by it.[157]

The record of debt and legal demands refers to the law. That is what Christ has nailed to the cross for us and tithing is part of the law. You cannot be tithing so it cannot be working. You have been lied to but because God sees your faithfulness, He has blessed you.

Common Argument Number Three - You're Just a Heresy Hunter

Yes. Yes, I am and it is a badge I wear with honor. The late heretic Paul Crouch tried desperately to turn the concept of a heresy hunter into a bad thing. Here is a direct quote:

"There's a spiritual application here. ... I want to say to all you scribes, pharisees, heresy-hunters, all of you that are around pickin' little bits of doctrinal error out of everybody's eyes and dividin' the Body of Christ ... get out of God's way, stop blockin' God's bridges, or God's goin' to shoot you if I don't ... let Him sort out all this doctrinal doodoo!"

So, God is going to shoot me? The reality is that the Bible clearly states it is false doctrine that causes the division in the church, not people correctly pointing it out. Paul Crouch spent his life promoting the worst false teachers alive. Their doctrines have sorely divided the church. Not the people calling them out as the Bible instructs us to do. The false teacher would love to leave the "doctrinal doodoo" up to God because they clearly do not believe in Him or fear Him. The amusing thing here is the mixing of scribes and

---

[155] **Trespass:** (Gr. *paraptōma*) This is a sin that can come in the way of some desire (lusting), some thinking (entertaining a wrongdoing) or some action (carrying out one's desires or thoughts that he or she has been entertaining) that is beyond or overstepping God's righteous standards, as set out in the Scriptures. It is falling or making a false step as opposed to standing or walking upright in harmony with the righteous requirements of God. – Matt. 6:14; Mark 11:25; Rom. 4:25; 5:15-20; 11:11; 2 Cor. 5:19; Gal. 6:1; Eph. 1:7; 2:1, 5; Col 2:13.

[156] σταυρός **stauros;** from the same as *2476;* an *upright stake,* hence a *cross* (the Rom. instrument of crucifixion): – cross (27). – NASB Dictionaries

[157] i.e. the cross; it could also be rendered *through him*

Pharisees, who were false, with heresy hunters who seek to expose what is false. It is illogical once again on its face.

I include this common argument because I have witnessed personally a distaste in many Christians for pointing out error. I have heard well-intended people say something similar to Crouch in that we should just "leave it all up to God." The New Testament is filled with so many scriptures about false teachers and preachers. It obviously meant a lot to God to make such an emphasis. At no place does He suggest we should just leave it all up to Him. Paul called out the false teachers of his day by name. The Bible says we are to mark them that cause division by presenting a different gospel. I have heard well-intended people just throw their hands up in the air and say those under deception do not want to hear the truth. I disagree for two reasons. First, I think some can come out from under deception if the true Gospel is preached to them enough and the falseness of what they sit under is exposed. Even if only a handful of the 45,000 weekly attendees of Joel Osteen's church come out and come to true penitent faith in Christ, isn't that worth it? The Bible says it is worth it:

Luke 15:7 Updated American Standard Version (UASV)

7 I tell you that in the same way, there will be more joy in heaven over one sinner who repents than over ninety-nine righteous persons who need no repentance.

We get so caught up in the megachurch mentality that we think one or two being saved is somehow a failure! There is a reason why Jesus says there is rejoicing when one sinner repents. He knows how difficult it is and how few truly answer the call. Remember, the way to the gate is narrow. Few find it. I saw recently a renowned false teacher claim his church had over 17,000 salvations in the previous year. No. You had 17,000 people you made repeat a two-sentence prayer, so you could plug them into their purpose serving your church. Far too many of them are still are on 'the way broad that leads to destruction, as opposed to 'the narrow way that leads to life. (Matt. 7:13-14) As David Platt said,

"Accept him? Do we really think Jesus needs our acceptance? Don't we need him? Jesus is no longer one to be accepted or invited in but one who is infinitely worthy of our immediate and total surrender." - David Platt

We have to get over ourselves and realize there are millions of people on the wrong side of salvation and the hourglass is running low. Many of those people sit next to us in church every week. You think listening to someone expose false teaching is too much for your delicate sensibilities? Try imagining hearing the screams of people when they stand before the Lord and realize they are in the wrong line. That should haunt us. Heresy hunter? You bet I am and proud of it.

Common Argument Number Four - You're Just Nitpicking

Truly I am not. I believe that reasonable people can disagree reasonably about things that are not central to doctrine. You're post tribulation, and someone else is pre-tribulation might be an interesting debate, but there is no heresy involved. I try to also go out of my way to make sure it is not just an error or an outlier. I remember seeing John Hagee once say something about God and money that was straight out of the prosperity gospel playbook. But it was one comment, in the 1990's, during a pledge drive. It would be unfair to label him a prosperity preacher because of one comment. He does, of course, believe in dual covenant theology that says the Jews do not need to come to Christ. He also worships Israel as an idol. He also recently told all of the atheists living in the US that they needed to leave "his country." But prosperity preacher? No. Likewise this year Brian Houston, prosperity preacher of Hillsong, was quoted in a sermon saying that Muslims and Christians serve the same God. Many ripped him and vilified him for it. I listened to the sermon, and while he did say it, I gave him the benefit of the doubt because he had never said something like that before. Sure, enough he clarified a few days later. It was just a mistake. He is still a huge heretic, but he does not believe in Chrislam.

Anyone can be in error. That is not the issue. Once your error has been pointed out however and you refuse to change it, you are no longer merely in error - now you are willfully false. Jesus likened it to leaven that will eventually spread through the entire batch. Look how many hundreds of thousands of people fell for the holy laughter nonsense out of Toronto in the 1990s? People rolling on the floor and barking like dogs? Completely demonic yet so many ran to embrace it. I prefer to talk about what we have in common, but you cannot call evil good. Light has no fellowship with darkness. Expel the evil brother from among you. People like Joel Osteen have tried to turn doctrine into a dirty word, but I assure you it is very important to God. Remember that John 1:1 says that Jesus is His Word. Thus, when you routinely lie about His Word you are lying about Him. You are bearing false witness against Christ Himself. That is no small deal.

CHAPTER FOURTEEN Assemblies of God Tithing Position

In the spirit of full disclosure, I was an Assemblies of God Minister. I was saved in an AG church. I was discipled there, took ministerial classes there and went through the credentialing process to become a reverend through the AG. I genuinely liked the Assemblies. They are not perfect but then again, no work of man ever can be. They had a good history of dealing with falseness properly. This was the organization that expelled Swaggart and Bakker, costing them millions of dollars for doing the right thing. They are however not without their blemishes such as Benny Hinn and the heretical Toronto Blessing, but people really do not understand AG. It is not a denomination. It is a collective of churches and the individual churches have the power. The only real power the assemblies have is over the individual credentials of their ministers but even if they pull them, ministers today continue on without them, just as I have. The AG did not call me to minister the Gospel, God did.

I was concerned with some of the direction the AG was heading in these end times. It seemed to waver about not embracing falseness as it should. They embraced the purpose driven deception years ago and more recently fully embraced the absolutely heretical book called The Circle Maker. A couple of years ago they held a luncheon honoring renowned false teacher/prophet Reinhard Bonnke. They continue to find themselves in bed with the likes of Christine Caine, Kenneth Copeland, Brian Houston and even Bill Johnson. The signs were not good, and as of two years ago, I returned my credentials to them. The Assemblies also are defenders of tithing, but that is to be expected. Nearly all of organized Christianity are defenders of tithing because it is what they know. It is what they have taught. They have their own biblical narrative, and they stick to it. There is probably a deep seeded fear that to renounce tithing would result in churches closing nationwide. As we move on in this chapter, I will respond to the official AG position on tithing. Their statement is italicized for contrast.

The Assemblies of God has always been a proponent of tithing (or giving one-tenth of one's personal income to support the work of God). We believe tithing is a recognition that everything we have comes from God. The practice checks our greed, promotes personal discipline and thrift, testifies to our faith, promotes God's work in the world, and alleviates human need. While we do not believe tithing to be a condition for salvation, we do believe it is a very important biblical model, one which should set the minimal standard for Christian giving for people in all income ranges. – AG Position Paper

We start off with the obvious that has already been proven scripturally throughout this book. Tithing was never income. Thus, the entire underpinning is false. It really is a shame because the New Testament model of giving is so close anyway. It is sad to see them cling to a two-thousand-year-old defunct agricultural system instead of simply relying on 2 Corinthians 9. Sowing and reaping. Cheerful giving. That is all recognizing that everything we have comes from God. There is simply no biblical reason to force a compulsory giving system when the Bible clearly says giving is now not to be under compulsion. There is no reason to subject the sheep back to the yoke of the law by pretending tithing is still in operation. Giving, in general, promotes personal discipline and thrift. Giving checks our greed testifies our faith and promotes the work of God in the world. It is an even grander testimony when it is not forced! Most church leaders will tell you that less than 20% of members tithe, to begin with, so the system does not work anyway! It is nice that AG does not consider tithing as a requirement for salvation, but it is borderline frightening that they would feel the need even to mention such a ghastly and irreverent thought. Tithing has already been proven not to be a New Testament biblical model at all and while it sounds good to say that it is the minimal standard for Christian giving that is simply not supported by God's Word. It shows a tremendous doubt in the work of the Holy Spirit inside believers. We continue with the statement:

"Though some people believe tithing was an Old Testament practice not intended for New Testament Christians, the Assemblies of God believes and teaches that tithing is still God's design for supporting the ministry and reaching the world with the gospel. Our bylaws state, "We recognize the duty of tithing and urge all our people to pay tithes to God" (Article IX, Section 7a.) It is true there is no direct commandment in the New Testament saying, "You must tithe to God one-tenth of your income"; but there is also no statement declaring the Old Testament plan as no longer valid." - AG Position Paper

As much as I like the Assemblies this is ridiculously ignorant of Galatians 5. I know we went over this, but I feel compelled to present it again:

Galatians 5:1-6 Updated American Standard Version (UASV)

5 For freedom Christ has set us free; stand firm therefore, and do not submit again to a yoke of slavery.

² Behold I, Paul, say to you that if you receive circumcision, Christ will be of no benefit to you. ³ And I testify again to every man who receives

circumcision, that he is under obligation to keep the whole law. ⁴ You are severed from Christ, you who would be[158] justified by the law; you have fallen away from grace. ⁵ For we through the Spirit, by faith, are waiting for the hope of righteousness. ⁶ For in Christ Jesus neither circumcision nor uncircumcision means anything, but faith working through love.

Do we really understand these Scriptures? When you force an Old Testament plan, which was part of the law, upon believers you place them back under the curse of the law. Christ is of no more advantage to them. Jesus Christ took the law and nailed it to the cross! Leave it there! We are free in Christ. Free to cheerfully give into the work of the kingdom! Will some people use that freedom to be stingy? Absolutely but I bet it is less than the current 20% that actually tithe! Not to mention the AG should know better what proper hermeneutics is. You do not create doctrine because there is no statement declaring the plan is no longer valid. The only thing that carried over from the Old Testament was the moral laws, and that was reiterated in the New Testament! How can you read the New Testament and think that the tithing command was not ended? Whenever Jesus mentioned tithing, it was a negative connotation. The parable of the tax collector and the Pharisee showed how much an idol it had become. 2Corinthians 9 outlines the new practice, eliminating the old. Why would God give us a new standard of giving if He intended the old to simply continue? Lastly, Galatians spells out in no uncertain terms that all parts of the law are done.

"Some oppose tithing today quoting Matthew 23:23 as proof text. In doing so they actually twist Jesus' words to teach just the opposite of what Jesus clearly said. "Woe to you, teachers of the law and Pharisees, you hypocrites! You give a tenth of your spices... But you have neglected the more important matters of the law—justice, mercy and faithfulness." Stopping at that point in the verse might allow some misinterpretation. But Jesus continued, "You should have practiced the latter, without neglecting the former." From here we see that Jesus regarded the Old Testament practice of tithing as continuing into the new covenant under which we now live." – AG Position Paper

Except of course the new covenant had not started yet. This kind of glaring error makes me doubt the sincerity of the beliefs. Jesus had not gone to the cross yet, so tithing was in effect still. No one is arguing that tithing was not a requirement for the Jewish people under the old covenant. Jesus did not nail the law and its requirements to the cross until He actually went to the cross. Secondly, however, Matthew 23:23 is a decent proof text. Jesus is mocking the Pharisees for their tithing practices! He is actually

---

[158] Or *are seeking* or *are attempting*

cursing them for it! He is showing them how their insistence on tithing had become an idol and a source of pride. This is hardly a ringing endorsement of tithing. Not to mention Jesus reinforcing a Jewish tradition of the law upon Jewish people does not bear any weight for New Testament believers! The larger point here though remains the fact that Christ had not yet gone to the cross so to say that He regarded tithing as continuing in the new covenant is flat out wrong.

"The practice of tithing predates the giving of the Old Testament law. Abraham tithed in response to God's blessing and faithfulness (Genesis 14:18-20) and was no doubt blessed because of his faithful tithing. Under the law, proceeds from the tithes were directed primarily for the support of the Levites and priests who provided religious leadership (Numbers 18:21-29) and for the relief of the needy (Deuteronomy 14:22-29). Today's church still relies on the support of tithers." – AG Position Paper

More things that are simply untrue. First of all, Abram (not Abraham) did not tithe in response to God's blessing and faithfulness. That is nowhere in the text. Most scholars agree it was probably the local pagan tradition. It is also a misrepresentation to claim that Abram "tithed." This is the same sleight of hand we see from abusive tithing teachers every week. When you say, someone tithed the clear inference you make is to the system of tithing which was not established until long after Abram walked the earth. Abram gave ten percent of the spoils of war, and the word for ten percent happens to be tithe. It is more honest to say that one time, Abram gave ten percent then to purposefully muddy the waters and pretend it had anything to do with the tithing system set up under the law.

There are other problems here though. The verses cited as proving Abram tithed in response to God's blessing and faithfulness are not the words of Abram at all. They are the words of Melchizedek. The impression given by the Assemblies here is that Genesis 14: 18-20 will support the notion that Abram tithed in response to God's blessing and faithfulness and those verses are not even words coming from Abram's mouth! The bigger problem here though is the notion that the Assemblies makes a declarative statement that is not supported in the text at all. To say that there is no doubt that Abram was blessed because of his faithful tithing is bizarre on many levels. First of all, we already know from the chapter before that God had already blessed Abram before this one-time tithing incident. We also know that God has already given him his promise of blessing and covenant for the future:

Genesis 13:2 Updated American Standard Version (UASV)

² Now Abram was very rich in livestock, in silver, and in gold.

FLEECING THE FLOCK

Genesis 12:1-3 Updated American Standard Version (UASV)

12 Now Jehovah said to Abram, "Go out from your land and from your relatives, and from the house of your father, to the land that I will show you. ² And I will make of you a great nation, and I will bless you and make your name great, so that you will be a blessing. ³ I will bless those who bless you, and him who curses you I will curse, and in you all the families of the earth shall be blessed."

There is no mention of tithing here beloved. Tithing has nothing to do with the level of blessedness Abram received. Abram was blessed because of his faithfulness and because of who God is. He was already wealthy before he gave a dime to Melchizedek. Also, when he did give the spoils of war to the king he gave nothing from his own considerable wealth so to pretend that this somehow sets up a new covenant principle is beyond a stretch. This is how desperate tithing teachers become. To state that a man who gave a tithe one time in a 175-year lifespan was "no doubt blessed by his faithful tithing" is simply deceptive.

At least the Assemblies is honest enough here to say they still rely upon the support of tithers but that does not mean it is biblical. The tithing system they speak of regarding the Levites was specifically for the management of the theocracy of Israel, not so Mega Church Pastor Bob can start a new building fund. Once again though I return to the pattern of New Testament giving and say that the church still can rely upon the generosity of the sheep. Once we stop fleecing them we may find out that God will indeed provide.

"Christians can miss out on God's abundant blessing by looking on the tithe as the entire requirement for giving. The tithe is only one aspect of support for the church and its ministry of spreading the gospel. The Bible also mentions voluntary offerings given by God's people over and above the required tithe. Of course, the attitude with which both tithes and offerings are given is very important. God loves a cheerful giver (2 Corinthians 9:7). The giving of either tithes or offerings with a grudging spirit loses much of the blessing that can come as we faithfully give out of love rather than obligation." – AG Position Paper

I really do not like the inferences to trying to motivate giving by tying it to blessings yet to come. By claiming you will miss out on abundant blessing if you only give a tithe. I give them the benefit of the doubt here but this is the same line of reasoning used by money grubbing televangelists. We spoke earlier about the Mike Murdocks and Paula Whites of the world who sell the blessings of God. We should really give out of a thankful heart for what God has already done.

"The Assemblies of God is also concerned about people who withhold tithes when they do not like decisions and directions espoused by spiritual

leaders. Christians should fellowship with a local body of believers and bring their whole tithes into that storehouse (Malachi 3:10). Though some of the Israelites may not have liked decisions made by Moses and his successors, they were given no alternatives. While we may designate some of our offerings (beyond the tithes) to ministries outside the local church, the tithes rightfully belong in the church with which the Christian identifies. And if one is not identifying with a local body of believers, he or she disregards God's instruction that we not forsake assembling together with believers (Hebrews 10:25)." – AG Position Paper

We went into great depth about the mishandling of Malachi 3. The storehouse mentioned there is not the modern-day church building. There is no point rehashing that, especially when there are so many other problems here:

1) Decisions and directions of leaders should be evaluated and if there is any suspicion that things are not of God you absolutely should withhold your money, lest you are paying into a work of darkness. We are to judge fruit. I know that the church likes to enforce a false authority paradigm but do not fall for it. That being said, if you know a church has gone rogue, you should not be staying there anyway. Move on and find someone preaching the uncompromised Gospel of Jesus Christ and sow into that ministry. By the way, I am not speaking about nitpicking decisions that were not given to us to make. I remember at my old church the pastor decided to help a church in Africa and I felt it was a mistake. I prayed, and I felt God say that was not a decision that was given to me. We have to be careful to not develop a critical spirit for the sake of being critical. In this day and age, everyone thinks they are an expert and everyone thinks they can make every decision. The pastor will answer for his decisions, and we will answer for ours. The issue is always doctrine. It is doctrine that saves people according to the pastoral letters of Paul. It is one of only two things Paul told Timothy to guard. We all have a responsibility to do the work of a Berean and if we find our church drifting into heresy and the leadership refuses accountability for it then we need to move on to where Christ and Him crucified is all that is preached. Do not sow into any work of darkness.

2) The comparison to Moses is illogical. Israel was a theocracy, and all the people knew Moses had been chosen by God. We know no such thing when it comes to the people in the pulpits today. God has given us plenty of choices today. Under this logic, if we attend a church that suddenly decides like Rob Bell did that there is no more hell and everyone is going to heaven we should just shut up and pay our tithes? How is that biblical at all? It is not.

3) The tithes do not rightfully belong to the church. That is arrogant to the point of sinful. Also, the church is not buildings with steeples. It is where any group of real believers in Christ gather. Sometimes those people meet in group settings instead of large buildings, and that is just as good and biblical. It is not forsaking the brethren. However, if you are alone, that is not good at all. We need other believers alongside us in this walk.

Ecclesiastes 4:9-12 Updated American Standard Version (UASV)

⁹ Two are better than one, because they have a good reward for their labor. ¹⁰ For if they fall, one will lift up his fellow. But woe to the one who falls when there is not another[159] to lift him up. ¹¹ Again, if two lie down together, they can keep warm, but how can one keep warm alone? ¹² And though a man might prevail against one who is alone, two will withstand him. A threefold cord is not quickly broken.

Just be wary of church worshippers. People who worship their church more than their God. People who advocate that only large arenas are where we should meet. That simply is not true. We conclude the Assemblies statement:

"Some Christians do not tithe, claiming they cannot afford to give up 10 percent of their income. Simple arithmetic may suggest that 90 percent will not go as far as 100 percent in satisfying essential family needs. But God has built a multiplication factor into our giving of tithes and offerings. Malachi recorded God's words, "Bring the whole tithe into the storehouse... Test me in this... and see if I will not throw open the floodgates of heaven and pour out so much blessing that you will not have room enough for it" (Malachi 3:10). Though we do not give to God in order to get more back, as some suggest we should, God's promises are still true–if our giving is according to His instruction." – AG Position Paper

Once again, the assemblies conclude by not understanding Malachi at all. Not understanding the reference to the law in Deuteronomy and the blessings and curses verses. The more disheartening thing is the clear doublespeak. This is textbook false prosperity tactics. "Though we don't give to God in order to get more" is offered as empty shallow piety compared to the opposing statements made in the same breath:

God has a multiplication factor built into our giving!

Test me in this!

I will throw open the floodgates of heaven!

---

[159] Lit *there is not a second*

I will pour you out so much blessings you will not have room!

God's promises remain true!

Assuming of course that you pay a tithing system that yokes you back to the slavery of the law. No, we don't give to get yet at the same time that is exactly what is being sold to the sheep. Hey, we don't give to get but wouldn't you like those floodgates thrown wide open for you? We do not give to get, but hey God said test Him because he has built in a multiplication factor into our giving! I might add here, what does that even mean? Where in the Bible does it say God has built in a multiplication factor into our giving? That sounds like Creflo Dollar wrote it. This is all classic prosperity gospel double-speak, and the Assemblies should be better than it.

What is wrong with simply saying that the most important work you can ever give your money to is the work of the kingdom of God? Real work of spreading the Gospel of Jesus Christ and bringing people to penitent faith in Christ for the forgiveness of their sins. That God saved us already and don't we have the burden Christ gave us for the lost? Do we have to tie giving to these earthly, carnal promises of "blessing" and basically arrange a quid-quo-pro with God? If you left giving up to the believer and the Holy Ghost you would be amazed at what your faith in God would result in. I think you would far exceed 20% of people giving and most of them would give more than the 10%. You have to be preaching the real Gospel though because only the real Gospel saves. A church full of goats that you are trying to teach to act like sheep requires a compulsory system like tithing. That doesn't make it any more right or biblical though. I like the Assemblies, but this statement is an accurate representation of many of the false tithing arguments wrapped up in exceptionally bad hermeneutics. Quite frankly, the AG should know better.

CHAPTER FIFTEEN The Hate the Church Lie

I feel compelled to address one ancillary lie that is coursing through the Christian bloodstream today as a result of the tithing lies and other abuses found in the church. That is the growing numbers of people shunning the fellowship and making an idol out of hating the organized church, usually due to some hurt they endured whether they admit to such or not. Those who follow my ministry know that I am not shy about chronicling the abuses in the church system today. I believe and demonstrate nearly every day that the majority of the church today is heading down the broad path that leads to destruction. Purpose driven church models, seeker friendly gospels, prosperity heresies, greasy grace antinomianism, CEO pastor models, false authority and tithing systems, and false prophetic models all combine to mislead so many people. Fake sinner's prayers, fake altar calls, and fake purposes all lead goats to believe they are sheep. Going to church every week but never in relationship with God. This is why so many will say "Lord, Lord" on the last day. I think sometimes we gloss past crucial Scriptures too easily:

Matthew 7:13-14 Updated American Standard Version (UASV)

[13] "Enter through the narrow gate; for the gate is wide and the way is broad that leads to destruction, and there are many who enter through it. [14] For the gate is small and the way is narrow that leads to life, and there are few who find it.

I know we all know the part that says, "narrow is the way" but we tend to stop reading before we get to the part that says "those who find it are few." Do we get that? Few. Not mega church numbers of people beloved. Few.

That said, I need to be clearer about something that has been weighing on my Spirit. I do not hate the church. I love the church. The church is the Bride of Christ. He gave His life for His church. We need to be very careful about throwing the baby out with the bathwater. Of being so righteously angry at false teachers that we start to think the entire institution is somehow evil. It is not. There are real sheep of God sitting in every church across this country. There are real shepherds of God leading churches across this country. I point out what is false, so they can come out from among that which is false. Not to tell them church as a whole is beyond redemption. I couldn't say that because it is biblically untrue. Just look at these verses.

Ephesians 5:25-27 Updated American Standard Version (UASV)

²⁵ Husbands, love your wives, just as Christ also loved the congregation[160] and gave himself up for her, ²⁶ so that He might sanctify her, having cleansed her by the washing of water with the word, ²⁷ that he might present the congregation[161] to himself in splendor, having no spot or wrinkle or any such thing; but that she might be holy and blameless.

Christ loved the church. He gave Himself up for her. He wants to sanctify her by the washing of His Word. He wants to present the church to Himself in splendor! And He will beloved. Make no mistake about it. We need to be very careful about what we say about the bride of our Lord and Savior. Our place is never to tear down what God has raised up. The Bible speaks of exposing false teaching, not being rebellious against the church as a whole. I would tread very carefully.

That leads us to the next logical question. Well, what was the church supposed to be? I have witnessed recently a lot of people who appear to be wounded from their church experiences and more sympathetic I could not be. Yet their defensiveness now seems targeted against anything in the church. It is a very dangerous spirit to be around because it is not the Spirit of the Lord. They point to Acts 2, where the church was established and claim it was met in homes. Let's see what the verses actually say:

Acts 2:42-47 Updated American Standard Version (UASV)

⁴² And they continued devoting themselves to the teaching of the apostles and to fellowship, to the breaking of bread and to prayers.[162] ⁴³ And fear came on every soul, and many wonders and signs were being performed through the apostles. ⁴⁴ And all those who believed were together and had all things in common; ⁴⁵ and they began selling their property and possessions and distributing these things to all, as anyone had need. ⁴⁶ Day by day continuing with one mind in the temple, and breaking bread from house to house, they were taking their food together with gladness and sincerity of heart, ⁴⁷ praising God and having favor with all the people. And the Lord added to their number day by day those who were being saved.

They broke bread in their homes and met corporately at the temple, reminding us that these first believers had come out of the Jewish culture. God does not want us alone, Satan does. Being with other believers by the

---

[160] Gr *ekklesia* ("assembly")
[161] Gr *ekklesia* ("assembly")
[162] Lit *the prayers*

way, does not include Facebook either. Those are fake relationships. Being part of a group on Facebook is not fellowship. Ecclesiastes teaches us this principle:

Ecclesiastes 4:9-12 Updated American Standard Version (UASV)

9 Two are better than one, because they have a good reward for their labor. 10 For if they fall, one will lift up his fellow. But woe to the one who falls when there is not another[163] to lift him up. 11 Again, if two lie down together, they can keep warm, but how can one keep warm alone? 12 And though a man might prevail against one who is alone, two will withstand him. A threefold cord is not quickly broken.

Can a church simply be a small gathering of believers? Absolutely. Do they have to meet in a big steepled building? Absolutely not. That does not mean however that they should not meet in big steepled buildings. In fact the Word of God seems to lean towards the public gatherings. There is also supposed to be an order to the church. The Bible makes things clear if we are willing to put aside our personal issues and admit it:

James 3:1 Updated American Standard Version (UASV)

3 Not many of you should become teachers, my brothers, knowing that we shall receive heavier judgment.

1 Timothy 5:17 Updated American Standard Version (UASV)

17 The elders who rule well are to be considered worthy of double honor, especially those who work hard in speaking[164] and teaching.

These first two Scriptures cannot be any plainer. For those who think everything is even in the church here is some unsettling news. It is not. We are all even in the eyes of God in that we are all sinners covered by the blood of Jesus, but that does not mean everyone is even in terms of what call and gifts they have. I am sure we all know people who fancy themselves teachers/preachers/pastors but cannot tell why the Message Bible is not fit for use. Or they readily dismiss centuries worth of solid Christian exposition under the guise of false piety. The truth according to the Word of God is that while everyone is charged with doing the work of a Berean, not everyone is called to divide the Word of Truth for the sheep. Not everyone is called to pastor, teach, or preach and those who are should receive double honor. The James verse actually says not many of us should even

---

[163] Lit *there is not a second*
[164] Or *preaching*

try to take on these roles because they then are held to a much higher standard. What standard? Let us turn to the Word:

1 Timothy 4:16 Updated American Standard Version (UASV)

[16] Pay close attention to yourself and to your teaching; persevere in these things, for as you do this you will ensure salvation both for yourself and for those who hear you.

Acts 20:26-27 Updated American Standard Version (UASV)

[26] Therefore, I testify[165] to you this day that I am innocent of[166] the blood of all men. [27] For I did not shrink from declaring to you the whole purpose of God.

The first verse is Paul speaking to his protégé Timothy as he prepares him for his role of pastor at Ephesus. I have heard people try to even say that fact, accepted for centuries, is also wrong. The pastoral letters are clear. Paul does not write to people telling them how to run a church for no particular reason. Hermeneutics does not mean you check your brain at the door. In this verse, he explicitly tells Timothy that the very salvation of his listeners is at stake when it comes to his preaching. That is why the standard is so high. That is why it is so disheartening to see false pastors today who do not care about the sheep entrusted to them by the Great Shepherd. They will be held to account for every sheep. The Acts verse is when Paul is saying goodbye to the Ephesian elders, and he basically admits here that if he had not preached the whole counsel of God, then those that would not be saved would be counted against him! Their blood, he would be responsible for! Think about that Mr. seeker friendly pastor! Before you go watering down the Gospel, you better beware. We have established scripturally that there are in fact leaders in the church. There is no question. It does not make them better. They should never lord their leadership over the sheep. I cringe when I see the modern church's obsession with chasing secular leadership principles when we have Christ! Jesus showed us that leadership is all about servanthood and humility. As Paul said; follow me as I follow Christ. There is a reason for this plan God has for organizing His church:

Ephesians 4:11-14 Updated American Standard Version (UASV)

[11] And he gave some as apostles, and some as prophets, and some as evangelists, and some as shepherds and teachers, [12] for the equipping of the holy ones or the work of ministry, to the building up of the body of

---

[165] Or *to bear witness*
[166] Lit *pure from*

Christ;[167] 13 until we all attain to the unity of the faith, and of the accurate knowledge[168] of the Son of God, to a mature man, to the measure of the stature which belongs to the fullness of Christ. 14 So that we may no longer be children, tossed to and fro by the waves and carried about by every wind of teaching, by the trickery of men, by craftiness with regard to the scheming of deceit;

God wants us to come to unity of the true faith and of the knowledge of the Son of God. He does not want us to be tossed about by every whim of doctrine that comes along. That is why there are overseers. That is why there are pastors. People charged with shepherding the flock and make sure none wander off. I have heard people recently say the entire role of pastor is unbiblical because the word never appears in Scripture. We cannot be this dense beloved. The word pastor comes from the Latin meaning shepherd. There is much human cunning, craftiness and deceitful schemes in the world and in the church. Too many are falling for this self-righteous trick of the devil where the very thing Christ died for has become the enemy. Are there gifts involved in these roles? Of course, so but the usage of the word "the" before apostles, prophets, evangelists and teachers indicates these are roles people are expected to hold. We turn to the Holman New Testament Commentary for more insight:

> **4:11.** This verse ties directly back to the last word of verse 7. Verse 11 picks up again the subject started in verse 7 to tell us the relationship between the call to unity and the spiritual gifts Christ has given us. Spiritual gifts are at the heart of Christ's strategy for building his church. The gifts are ministers (or ministries) for the church. While this issue is strongly debated, particularly by Pentecostal and charismatic theologians, evangelical doctrine has traditionally held that of those four gifts two of them are still in existence and two have passed away. These gifts will be looked at more closely in the "Deeper Discoveries" section. For now, it is adequate to make the observation that the apostles and prophets seem no longer to be part of God's work in the church. The church was laid on the foundation of the ministry of the apostles and prophets (Eph. 2:20). Now that that foundation has been laid, the evangelists and the pastor-teachers are being used by God to build the superstructure.

---

[167] **Body of Christ (Congregation):** (Gr. *sōma tou Christou*) Metaphorically, the phrase refers to all persons who are an anointed born again member of the Christian congregation as a whole.–Rom. 12:15; 1 Cor. 12:12-20, 22-25; Eph. 4:12, 16.

[168] *Epignosis* is a strengthened or intensified form of *gnosis* (*epi*, meaning "additional"), meaning, "true," "real," "full," "complete" or "accurate," depending upon the context. Paul and Peter alone use *epignosis*.

4:12. It is not the task of these gifted people to do all the work of the ministry. Their task is to **prepare God's people for works of service.** When believers are equipped and people accept the adventure of ministering to others, then the whole body is built up, matured, strengthened, and flourishes.

4:13. Diverse gifts create and build up one body in unity. This unity is in faith and knowledge of Christ. Christ does not try to build up superstars in his kingdom with superior faith or superior knowledge. He tries to build up a church unified in its faith and knowledge, each member being built up to maturity. All are to reach the **fullness of Christ.** The church's goal is that each member and thus the entire church will show to the world all the attributes and qualities of Christ. Then the church will truly be the one body of Christ.

4:14–16. The result of these spiritually gifted people's equipping the saints is that believers are not to be like children, easily persuaded and confused, jumping from one opinion or belief to the next, like **waves** on the sea being driven by gusting winds of false **teaching.** Rather, the believers are to speaking the truth in love. Speaking the truth in love is a mark of maturity, which will enable us to grow up spiritually. Immature people often fall into one of two opposite errors. They speak the truth, but without love, or they love without speaking the truth. When we do the first, we often brutalize others, pounding them with truth but doing it in an unloving way. When we do the second, we don't tell others the truth, thinking that by shielding them from the truth we are sparing them from pain. We are not, however. All we are doing is delaying their maturation. To share the truth with our fellow believers is a mark of maturity, but to do it with love, with understanding, with compassion. From Christ the whole body is gifted, and as each one uses his gift for the benefit of others, the whole body matures. We must recognize that we belong to one another, we need one another, no matter how insignificant we think our contribution is. There are no little people in the kingdom of God, as Francis Shaeffer used to say, and there are no little jobs. Just as a physical body needs red corpuscles and livers more than it needs a handsome face or beautiful hair, so we all belong; we are all necessary. We all can contribute, and when we do, we all grow to maturity in Christ.

4:14. The Ephesian church, as most of the churches Paul wrote, faced teachers with opposing viewpoints. They divided the church body into factions, each opposing the others. Their presence required the type of spiritual maturity and church unity Paul had described. Without such unity the church would act like a group of babies, each crying out because

> of his own pains and needs, each inconsistently saying one thing and then another, each at the mercy of cunning, deceitful teachers. To avoid infantile behavior, the church must mature into unity of the faith and of knowledge of Christ.[169]

The reality is the New Testament is loaded with instruction for how the church should be organized and the separation of roles within it. That may chafe against us, but it is only our flesh which rebels. I am not speaking about blindly following any man but if my pastor preaches the whole Gospel and lives a life that says follow me as I follow Christ; count me in.

1 Peter 5:1-5 Updated American Standard Version (UASV)

5 Therefore, I exhort the elders among you, as your fellow elder and witness of the sufferings of Christ, and a partaker also of the glory that is to be revealed, ² shepherd the flock of God among you, exercising oversight not under compulsion, but willingly, according to the will of God; and not for sordid gain, but with eagerness; ³ nor yet as lording it over those allotted to your charge, but becoming examples to the flock. ⁴ And when the chief Shepherd appears, you will receive the unfading crown of glory. ⁵ In the same way, you younger men, be in subjection to the elders; and all of you clothe yourselves with humility toward one another, for God opposes the proud, but he gives grace to the humble ones.

That sure sounds a lot like order beloved. Shepherd the flock. Exercise oversight willingly. Not for shameful gain, which disqualifies many today. Not domineering over those in your charge; that disqualifies even more. Being what to the flock? An equal? No, an example. Clothe yourself in humility. It is not about being different, but not everyone is called to do the same thing. Christ wants His Bride to grow in maturity; not be tossed around by every new wave of doctrine because they have no leader. Without the shepherd/pastor/teacher, we become a rudderless boat, drifting this way and that. I have seen it too. I have seen the result of false teaching that drives Christians into these walled communities where they just cast stones at the church while rummaging through Scriptures they do not understand. Does the Holy Spirit lead us into all truth? Of course, but sometimes we do not see the truth for what it is. Sometimes God can give different revelations and sometimes we may not see at all. There is no shame in knowing people who know more than you. I have people I can email and ask a question about Scripture that might be tripping me up, and

---

[169] Max Anders, *Galatians-Colossians*, vol. 8, Holman New Testament Commentary (Nashville, TN: Broadman & Holman Publishers, 1999), 152–153.

I do not mean people who will tell me what I want to hear. The day we think we are beyond that is the day we are no longer teachable.

Even though there is much wrong in the church today, it should come as no surprise since God warned us about this throughout the New Testament. Yet even in these churches are the real sheep of God. It is so disappointing sometimes to listen to people who have been clearly hurt but refuse to acknowledge it. They dismiss thousands of years of biblical interpretation and research because they think they have the only revelation that matters. People who seem to react in glee whenever something goes wrong in the church. People who seem to root for things to go wrong in the church. Recently, for example, we saw the Acts 29 Network disassociate themselves from Mark Driscoll and Mars Hill Church. It was long overdue. I have documented the abuses of Driscoll for years now. But this was not a happy day. When someone who started out trying to serve God loses his way over a period of ten years, we should not be rejoicing. I am happy for the sheep because maybe now they can get a pastor who will stick to the Gospel alone. But I weep for the church because she is the bride of Christ and she suffered throughout this story. I pray Mark Driscoll genuinely repents and seeks forgiveness. Christ forgave us. We ought to be waiting to forgive people; not waiting to cast that first stone.

I say that because it becomes really easy to do nothing but complain. It becomes really easy to sit behind a computer screen and hurl rocks at the church. They make an easy target; no doubt. It has to transcend that because there is no mercy in it. Now hear me out. I have no mercy for the wolves who are attacking the flock of God. I will expose them with every breath within me because they are killing the sheep, whether they intend to or not. Wrath, however, is when we only look at the wolves. Anger, bitterness, even righteous indignation; all when our eyes are fixed on the wolf. The problem is that there are still the sheep to consider. When we focus on them we find mercy, or at least we should. I have heard many Christians essentially say, "to hell with them." If they are too stupid to continue to sit under false teaching, there is nothing we can do about it. That is simply not how I interpret the parable of the 99 and 1. All sheep are precious to God. We preach the Word without compromise, expose what is false, and mercifully keep our eyes on His sheep.

Because whether we like it or not, the church is His Bride. So many Christians today stand around the Bride of Christ with rocks in their hands and call her a whore. They feel perfectly justified in casting the first stone. They think that all of Christendom for centuries have been wrong, but they have it all figured out. The arrogance is staggering in its sinfulness. I openly admit I do not have it all figured out at all. I am a wretch telling people about a God that saves wretches. Drop the stones beloved and realize that the church we look upon with such disdain is still His bride. He still is sanctifying it. He still wants to wash it clean with His Word and present it unto Himself. Be very careful what you hold in such contempt, lest it becomes an idol unto you. Be very careful indeed.

CHAPTER SIXTEEN A Way Forward

It is difficult sometimes to accept such a radical departure from everything we have been taught. I understand that. I was raised Catholic, where giving was not only the norm, but it was strictly enforced. I drifted into the world for many years before being saved from the pit my life had become by Jesus Christ in 2002. That was in a Pentecostal Assemblies of God church. Comparatively, the AG experience is vastly different from the Catholic experience. I was not used to people being happy during church. I was not used to all the singing and dancing, let alone the free expression of the gifts of the Spirit. I had to unlearn some bad teaching and relearn new theology. The great difference between the two is that the Catholic church-bred dependence upon the church and not God. We were never encouraged to read the Bible for ourselves, and many Catholic churches discourage it. In the AG church, however, personal growth and learning to foster your relationship with God through the reading of His Word was the norm. Over the years in my church and by taking ministerial classes I grew not only in the Word but drew closer to God as a result. I began to learn how to apply correct hermeneutics; a fancy word for Bible interpretation.

This developing closeness with God and better understanding of His Word inevitably led me to some conclusions about the denomination I found myself in. It reminded me about the scene from the secular movie the Seventh Sign where a young Jewish boy is having a conversation with a Catholic priest about who goes to heaven. The boy says (paraphrasing) that the Christian doesn't think it will be the Muslim, the Muslim doesn't think it will be the Jew and the Jew doesn't think it will be the Buddhist. What if we are all wrong? I say that merely to note that I think we are all wrong. I think it is the height of human arrogance to think he has figured out everything about God.

Isaiah 55:8-9 Updated American Standard Version (UASV)

8 For my thoughts are not your thoughts,
  neither are your ways my ways, declares Jehovah.
9 For as the heavens are higher than the earth,
  so are my ways higher than your ways
  and my thoughts than your thoughts.

The ways of God are infinitely higher than our ways, yet we think that the way we choose to worship Him is the way He intended. No theology is perfect because at the end of the day it is imperfect man trying to define a perfect God. Through using His Word alone, the best we can do is clearly identify what is false and try our level best to continue to improve our own walk. Yet as I was learning I began to realize that even within this great church where I was saved, some things were not squaring with the Bible. It was obvious to me that the majority of the gifts were being handled wrongly, but that is a story for another book. There seemed to be a very narcissistic spirit. I tithed of course because that was what I was taught and it only made sense the way it was taught. I was blessed to have a pastor that never abused tithing and never even wanted to know what anyone's giving pattern was like. It was between God and us, as it should be. As I continued to grow and watch more Christian television and online Christian programming, I noticed however that the vast majority of Christian leaders preached a much harsher tithing message that drove me back into Scripture to try and understand better. Then came the night with Bishop Ken McNatt and my life was forever changed. My understanding was forever changed. Up to that point, I was still horribly naïve. I assumed everyone was in this for Jesus but after that night, with the altar of my church covered in filthy lucre, my eyes were opened. The little dog had pulled back the curtain, and I saw the wizard for what he really was. From that night forward, my discernment grew. I started listening to sermons as a Berean would; eagerly seeing if everything lined up with Scripture.

    I say all of this because I understand where a lot of people might be as they wind down reading this book. I understand what it is like to have all of your foundational underpinnings ripped away from you. To realize that some people in the church leadership have lied to you. Perhaps some have not lied but were merely deceived themselves. That is an important distinction I need to make before this book closes. I refer throughout this book to the lies that are told regarding tithing. I do not mean to paint everyone with the same brush. A lie is often defined as a willful act of deception. I do not mean to infer that everyone who preaches tithing is willfully deceiving you. Some are themselves deceived, as we showed earlier in the book. The result, however, is the same. False teaching is false teaching regardless of our intent. God is not going to care that we had good intentions while abusing His sheep. He gave us His Word for a reason. That is so when we do our work and only care what God has to say, you must conclude that tithing is simply not for New Testament believers.

    I know that is difficult for many to swallow because it has been so ingrained in you, but the Word of God has to be our arbiter, not our feelings. The proof in Galatians alone should make us run from tithing. The fact that we are in danger of falling back under the curse of the law? We cannot say we have been saved by the grace of Jesus Christ and then insist on being held under the yoke of the law when it comes to giving. I am sorry but when you truly examine the tithing arguments they just have no

Biblical substance to them. There is no denying that the tithing system was developed as part of the Mosaic Law. The same law that was nailed to the cross to set us free. Tithing was not part of the moral code, which carried over. It was part of the civil code for the organization of the theocracy of Israel. It was implemented so the Levites would have food. Not everyone even had to tithe. Only those who produced agriculture. The poor certainly never tithed. Jesus never tithed because He was a craftsman.

The usage of Malachi must be one of the most egregious examples of eisegesis ever perpetrated. People who want to demand tithing read into the text what they want. They take four verses of a book that has four chapters, rip them violently out of context and demand that it institutes a universal principle. Despite the fact that God was talking to the priests, not the people. Despite the fact that New Testament believers cannot be placed under a curse. Despite the fact that the reference to throwing open the floodgates of heaven is a reference back to Deuteronomy 28 and the blessings and curses associated with keeping the entire law, which no one could ever do. Despite the fact that the tithe was never about money or income. Despite the fact that the storehouse cannot possibly mean the church of today. Despite all of these facts, the tithing preacher will still go out this Sunday and tell the sheep of God that they are robbing the Lord. That they rob Him in tithes and offerings. That they will be cursed because of it. That God wants so badly to shower them with untold blessings if they would stop being so darn cheap. All of it are lies, whether intentional or otherwise.

Or they will turn to Abram and Jacob and say that they "tithed," which they most certainly did not. To say someone "tithed" is to make a clear inference to the tithing system, which was not present during the life of either man. The case for Abram is that one time in a lifespan of 175 years he gave ten percent of the spoils of war to a pagan king as was the custom. Then, in fact, he gave the remaining 90% as well. He never gave one dime of his own wealth, which was substantial. He never did this again for the rest of his life and had not done it prior. The case for Jacob is even flimsier. Jacob shows no faith whatsoever in God by saying he will give ten percent if God delivers a certain level of blessedness unto him. There is actually no proof anywhere that Jacob ever did follow through on this promise, so you cannot even say he ever gave ten percent, ever. Even if he did, it is again a onetime incident in a lifespan of 147 years. Yet the tithing teachers want us to believe that these two incidents establish some sort of "universal principle" about you giving them the first 10% of your income. Think about the utter absurdity of that thought process. They want you to believe that God wanted us to understand there was a universal principle regarding the giving of the first ten percent of our income yet for some reason He waited about 2500 years before He established it in the Mosaic Law. During those 2500 years, there are only two mentions of a tenth being given. One time it was to a local pagan king from the spoils of war, and the other time He does not bother to even verify in His Word that it ever actually occurred. It is beyond ridiculous to then assert a universal principle. In desperation, they will then turn to stories such as Cain and Abel or even Adam and Eve, but they find no Biblical proof there. Thinking the tree of the Knowledge of Good and Evil represents the tithe makes no sense biblically, mathematically, or logically. As for Cain and Abel, the Bible teaches us that Abel's offering was better because of the faith in which it was presented, not because it was first fruits and Cain's was of lesser quality.

The bottom line is we have covered all of the deceptions in this book and debunked all of them. From the horrendous lie that Jesus taught tithing to the very clever first fruits lie. Now the question is what is the way forward? Where do we go from here? Let me first start with those who find themselves in the preaching/pastoral profession. You have to stop preaching and teaching tithing. I know it will require great faith on your part to step out, but we serve a great God. If you are truly preaching the Gospel and bringing people to penitent faith in Christ, then you will be amazed at what God will provide through the accurate preaching of His Word and the indwelt Holy Spirit amongst your sheep. If you are not preaching the true Gospel, however we have a bigger problem. It does not matter if you preach tithing or not until you first get off of the purpose driven bandwagon. You are not the CEO. The Bride of Christ is not a business. Stop chasing secular leadership principles. Stop thinking it is your responsibility to fill the pews. It is your responsibility to preach the Gospel. It does not need to be dressed up, watered down, made extra sugary or extra relevant to a dying culture. You do not need to figure anything out about it at all. You just need to preach it. Once you do, preach New Testament giving and not the yoke of the law. Hear me well, if the offerings you take suddenly drop, then that is the resources God has entrusted with you. The vision belongs to God, not you. No one has asked you to cast a vision other than the Bible. If your offerings dramatically increase, then God will want to see your faithfulness with the resources He has given you. Either way, preach the Gospel, feed the sheep, and let God decide who is added to the flock.

For the sheep, however, the way forward begins with your accepting the truth. None of these lies excuses not giving into the work of God. The verses in 2 Corinthians 9 are a higher standard:

2 Corinthians 9:6-7 Updated American Standard Version (UASV)

⁶ Now as to this, he who sows sparingly will also reap sparingly, and he who sows bountifully will also reap bountifully. ⁷ Each one must give

as he has decided in his heart, not reluctantly or under compulsion, for God loves a cheerful giver.

We must always remember the true universal principle of giving. Sowing and reaping. If we are in a good church, with a Gospel-centric pastor who does not compromise, then we will find no better place to sow our money into. The higher standard, however, has you in charge of it. It demands that you are not reluctant but rather that you willingly give your money cheerfully. That brings us however to the unspoken reality. What if you are in a church that is not good? I am not one to tell people to leave churches because I know how hard it is to find a good church. There are several considerations here. First of all, if you are in a church that does not present the full Gospel. Waters it down and sweetens it up. Refuses to talk about sin and repentance. The sinner's prayer is some diabetic nonsense about inviting Jesus into your heart but no frank discussion why we need a Savior. If this is the case, I am afraid that you do need to leave. You certainly should not be sowing money into a ministry like that because then you partner with the work of darkness.

Yes, I said that right. If you have a church like I just described it is a work of darkness. I cannot imagine a more obvious work of darkness. To imitate a work of God. To imitate a move of God. To draw people in for the sole reason of giving them a fake altar call with a fake sinner's prayer so you can then plug them into a ministry? Yes beloved. That is evil. Why? Because how many of them will stand before the Lord unsaved, being deceived their whole life?

Matthew 7:21-23 Updated American Standard Version (UASV)

²¹ "Not everyone who says to me, 'Lord, Lord,' will enter the kingdom of heaven, but the one who does the will of my Father who is in heaven. ²² On that day many will say to me, 'Lord, Lord, did we not prophesy in your name, and cast out demons in your name, and do many mighty works in your name?' ²³ And then I will declare to them, 'I never knew you; depart from me, you who practice lawlessness.'

Lord, Lord, did we not go to Saddleback or Lakewood church for decades? Did we not serve in the security ministry for decades? Did we not find our purpose? He will say away from me. Can some people find God in churches such as these? Absolutely because God is not hard to find if you are genuinely looking for Him. They are the exception though, not the norm. So, if you find yourself in one of these churches, I am afraid it is time to leave and find a church preaching the whole Gospel. It may not be as big. It may not be as pretty. Those are all irrelevant adornments. Broad is the path the leads to destruction. Few find the way to eternal life.

Popularity amongst the world, is not a sign that God is blessing and approving. If you want, try to speak to the pastor about your concerns. My guess is you will be met with no desire to learn. You will be corrected and dismissed. It is time to leave.

Now, if you are in a good church with a gospel-centric pastor who refuses to compromise, that is more important than the tithing issue in my opinion. Go and talk to him about tithing. Show him the Scriptures, see what he says. Sometimes we get caught up in the idea of perfect doctrine, and it is never going to happen. We need to make a stand for the purity of the Gospel but if some of the side stuff is not quite to our liking that does not mean we should be running for the hills. Now, tithing is not side stuff if it is being abused. If the pastor uses it to lord himself over the sheep, to beat up the sheep with guilt, pronounce curses or any of the things we discussed here then I do think it is time to at least have a chat with him. By the way, if your pastor is incapable of finding time to speak to one of his sheep, then he is not a pastor at all. That is part of the damage the CEO pastor role and the purpose driven church inflicts upon the flock of God.

The most important thing is you now know the truth. You have examined the Scriptures for yourself. You see the folly in pretending Abram tithed. You understand that Jesus had not gone to the cross yet when He told the Pharisees they should tithe. You understand Malachi as God intended you to; as an entire book. These are important details for you in your walk. No one can ever pull the wool over your eyes again when it comes to giving. You will be able to spot that seed-sowing, snake oil salesman the minute he goes into his sales pitch. You can now partner with God and His indwelt Holy Spirit to cheerfully give into the work of the kingdom. No more reluctance. No more wondering. It is no wonder because the truth of God's Word always sets you free. Do not waste that freedom. Tell others and spread the good news of the Good News. Christ died to set us free. Free from the shackles of financial heresy. Free from the wolves who seek to devour us. The Bible says that His people perish because of a lack of knowledge. The knowledge they are referring to is the Word of God. We do perish without knowledge. Without understanding what God has to say. Now you know what God has to say on the subject of giving and tithing. God bless you in your walk with Him, keeping Him first in everything we do. For His glory and His glory alone. In Jesus mighty name. Amen.

Bibliography

A., M. E., Harris, R. L., Archer Jr., G. L., & Waltke, B. K. (1999). *Theological Wordbook of the Old Testament.* Chicago: Moody Press.

Akin, D. L. (2001). *The New American Commentary: 1, 2, 3 John.* Nashville, TN: Broadman & Holman.

Alden, R. L. (2001). *Job, The New American Commentary, vol. 11.* Nashville: Broadman & Holman Publishers.

Anders, M. (2005). *Holman Old Testament Commentary - Proverbs.* Nashville: B&H Publishing.

Anders, M., & Butler, T. (2002). *Holman Old Testament Commentary: Isaiah.* Nashiville, TN: B&H Publishing.

Anders, M., & Lawson, S. (2004). *Holman Old Testament Commentary - Psalms: 11.* Grand Rapids: B&H Publishing.

Anders, M., & McIntosh, D. (2009). *Holman Old Testament Commentary - Deuteronomy.* Nashville: B&H Publishing.

Barker, K. L., & Bailey, W. (2001). *The New American Commentary: vol. 20, Micah, Nahum, Habakkuk, Zephaniah.* Nashville, TN: Broadman & Holman Publishers.

Bercot, D. W. (1998). *A Dictionary of Early Christian Beliefs.* Peabody: Hendrickson.

Blomberg, C. (1992). *The New American Commentary: Matthew.* Nashville, TN: Broadman & Holman Publishers.

Borchert, G. L. (2001). *The New American Commentary: John 1-11.* Nashville, TN: Broadman & Holman Publishers.

Borchert, G. L. (2002). *The New American Commentary vol. 25B, John 12–21.* Nashville: Broadman & Holman Publishers.

Brand, C., Draper, C., & Archie, E. (2003). *Holman Illustrated Bible Dictionary: Revised, Updated and Expanded.* Nashville, TN: Holman.

Breneman, M. (1993). *The New American Commentary, vol. 10, Ezra, Nehemiah, Esther.* Nashville: Broadman & Holman Publishers.

Brooks, J. A. (1992). *The New American Commentary: Mark (Volume 23)*. Nashville: Broadman & Holman Publishers.

Butler, T. C. (2005). *Holman Old Testament Commentary - Hosea, Joel, Amos, Obadiah, Jonah, Micah* . Nashville: Broadman & Holman Publishers.

Christiaan, E. (2015). *TITHING: Exposing One Of The Biggest Lies In The Church*. New York, NY: BookPatch LLC.

Cole, R. D. (2000). *THE NEW AMERICAN COMMENTARY: Volume 3b Numbers*. Nashville: Broadman & Holman Publishers.

Croteau, D. A. (2001). *Perspectives on Tithing: Four Views*. Nashville, TN: B&H Academic.

Elwell, W. A. (2001). *Evangelical Dictionary of Theology (Second Edition)*. Grand Rapids: Baker Academic.

Elwell, W. A., & Beitzel, B. J. (1988). *Baker Encyclopedia of the Bible*. Grand Rapids, MI: Baker Book House.

Garrett, D. A. (1993). *Proverbs, Ecclesiastes, Song of Songs, The New American Commentary, vol. 14*. Nashville: Broadman & Holman Publishers.

Garrett, D. A. (1993). *The New American Commentary: Vol. 14 (Proverbs, Ecclesiastes, Song of Songs)*. Nashville: Broadman & Holman Publishers.

George, T. (2001). *The New American Commentary: Galatians* . Nashville, TN: Broadman & Holman Publishers.

Hill, E. M. (2010). *What Preachers Never Tell You About Tithes & Offerings: The End of Clergy Manipulation & Extortion*. Atlanta, GA: SunHill Publishers.

Jameson, T. (2016). *The Tithing Conspiracy: Exposing the Lies & False Teachings About Tithing and the Prosperity Gospel*. Carrollton, GA: Inspired Word Publishers.

Lea, T. D., & Griffin, H. P. (1992). *The New American Commentary, vol. 34, 1, 2 Timothy, Titus*. Nashville: Broadman & Holman Publishers.

Martin, D. M. (2001, c1995). *The New American Commentary 33 1, 2 Thessalonians* . Nashville, TN: Broadman & Holman.

Martin, G. S. (2002). *Holman Old Testament Commentary: Numbers*. Nashville: Broadman & Holman Publishers.

Mathews, K. A. (2001). *The New American Commentary vol. 1A, Genesis 1-11:26* . Nashville: Broadman & Holman Publishers.

Matthews, K. A. (2001). *The New American Commentary Vol. 1B, Genesis 11:27-50:26.* Nashville: Broadman and Holman Publishers.

Melick, R. R. (2001). *The New American Commentary: Philippians, Colossians, Philemon, electronic ed., Logos Library System.* Nashville: Broadman & Holman Publishers.

Melick, R. R. (2001). *The New American Commentary: vol. 32, Philippians, Colissians, Philemon.* Nashville, TN : Broadman & Holman Publishers.

Morris, L. (1992). *The Gospel According to Matthew, The Pillar New Testament Commentary.* Grand Rapids, MI(; Leicester, England: W.B. Eerdmans; Inter-Varsity Press,.

Mounce, R. H. (2001, c1995). *Romans: The New American Commentary 27.* Nashville: Broadman & Holman.

Mounce, W. D. (2006). *Mounce's Complete Expository Dictionary of Old & New Testament Words.* Grand Rapids, MI: Zondervan.

Polhill, J. B. (2001). *The New American Commentary 26: Acts.* Nashville: Broadman & Holman Publishers.

Renee, R., & Harper, C. (2014). *The Tithing Hoax: Exposing the Lies, Misinterpretations & False Teachings about Tithing.* Morrisville, NC: LuLu Press.

Richardson, K. (1997). *The New American Commentary Vol. 36 James.* Nashville: Broadman & Holman Publishers.

Robertson, N. (2008). *Tithing : God's Financial Plan.* Matthews, NC: Norman Robertson Media.

Rooker, M. F. (2000). *The New American Commentary, vol. 3A, Leviticus.* Nashville: Broadman & Holman Publishers.

Schreiner, T. R. (2003). *The New American Commentary: 1, 2 Peter, Jude.* Nashville: Broadman & Holman.

Smith, G. (2007). *The New American Commentary: Isaiah 1-39, Vol. 15a.* Nashville, TN: B & H Publishing Group.

Smith, G. (2009). *The New American Commentary: Isaiah 40-66, Vol. 15b.* Nashville, TN: B&H Publishing.

Stein, R. H. (2001, c1992). *The New American Commentary: Luke.* Nashville, TN: Broadman & Holman .

Stuart, D. K. (2006). *The New American Commentary: An Exegetical Theological Exposition of Holy Scripture EXODUS.* Nashville: Broadman & Holman.

Taylor, R. A., & Clendenen, R. E. (2007). *The New American Commentary: Haggai, Malachi, , vol. 21A .* Nashville, TN: Broadman & Holman Publishers.

Vine, W. E., Unger, M. F., & White Jr., W. (1996). *Vine's Complete Expository Dictionary of Old and New Testament Words.* Nashville, TN: T. Nelson.

Vunderink, R. W., & Bromiley, G. W. (1979–1988). *The International Standard Bible Encyclopedia, Revised (,* . Grand Rapids, MI: Wm. B. Eerdmans.

Warren, R. (2002). *The Purpose Driven Life: What on Earth Am I Here For?* Grand Rapids: Zondervan.

Wells, A. B. (2007). *Tithing: Nailed To The Cross.* Bloomington, IN: Author House.

Wood, D. R. (1996). *New Bible Dictionary (Third Edition).* Downers Grove: InterVarsity Press.